Sport Fish
of the
Atlantic

Also From Florida Sportsman:
Baits, Rigs & Tackle
From Hook to Table
Fishing Planner
Sport Fish of Florida
Sport Fish of the Gulf of Mexico

Florida Sportsman Magazine
Florida Sportsman Fishing Charts
Lawstick Law Guides

Edited by Eric Wickstrom
Art Direction by Karen Miller
Copy Edited by Jerry McBride

ISBN 0-936240-17-2

Sport Fish of the Atlantic

By Vic Dunaway

Original Illustrations by
Kevin R. Brant

www.floridasportsman.com/books

Sport Fish of the Atlantic

CONTENTS

Preface

Stretching Your Limit

For a fisherman on the prowl, here's your essential bar-hopping guide.

By bars, of course, we refer to those countless banks, rocks and shallow areas where gamefish of all types and sizes await your baits and lures.

Sport Fish of the Atlantic identifies the many popular residents of those alluring bars and goes on to deeper waters where you may well encounter fabled giants such as great white sharks, blue marlin, giant tuna and billfish.

Battle them all. Know who they are.

What is that fish on the end of your line? Is it good to eat? What tackle should you use? How big do they get?

Those are key questions every angler asks. Now you have the answers in one compact volume written by an expert author and fisherman who learned during a half-century on the water. Each fish is shown in original illustrations meticulously painted for this book.

This is no textbook for a classroom exploration of the hundreds of thousands of species out there that go mostly unseen by the typical person.

Instead, you have here a practical guide covering every species you'll likely see along the most fascinating stretch of angling ocean on our planet. Hot and cold, the Atlantic waters offer it all.

Take this paper buddy along as the fishing companion you'll find valuable year after year.

Bar hopping never was more productive.

—*Karl Wickstrom*

Publisher

Here's the salty stage where an angler's dream team of fishing stars swim and battle, all the popular species off North America's Atlantic coast, from stripers and snook to marlin and tarpon.

Nova
Scotia

• New York

• Norfolk

Bermuda •

CONTINENTAL SHELF

Sport Fish of the Atlantic

Jacksonville •

Gulf Stream

Miami •

Bahamas

The Atlantic Coast

FISHING THE ATLANTIC COAST

As the seagull flies, North America's Atlantic Coast stretches for more than 3,000 miles, and when you measure in all the nooks and crannies—or, more nautically, all the bays, coves and estuaries—the actual distance increases by more than 10 times.

Productive saltwater fishing of one kind or another can be found in virtually every one of those miles, starting at the subarctic shores of Canada's Northern Quebec and ending on the subtropical flats of the Florida Keys. This being a book about sport fishing rather than geography, that will be the extent of the "Atlantic Coast" as covered in these pages, and outlined as follows.

The reader should note that the species of fish mentioned in the survey are merely the most popular or prominent ones in each area covered. Many others are available for the catching as well, and nearly all of them are illustrated and described in the book's main section.

ATLANTIC CANADA

Geographically, the Eastern Shore of huge and icy Baffin Island, which lies across the Hudson Strait from Labrador and Quebec, is no doubt a northward extension of the Atlantic Coast. But not from an angler's viewpoint. The bays of Baffin Island do contain plenty of Arctic Char, true, but up there you'll find too few facilities to allow for a thriving sport fishery. Also too many polar bears. Unlike the brown bears of Alaska—which can be dangerous in certain circumstances but are too wary to stalk interloping fishermen for food—the polar bears of Baffin Island see few people and those they do encounter are likely to be viewed more as groceries than as curiosities.

For practical purposes, then, northern Atlantic Coast angling starts at Ungava Bay in Northern Quebec, where enterprising outfitters have opened up some sensational tidewater fishing for Arctic Char.

Fishing facilities multiply rapidly as the sportsman works southward along the coast of Labrador, which is the mainland portion of the Province of Newfoundland. While freshwater fishing is the big draw in

Labrador, sea-run Trout and Atlantic Salmon are taken along the coast.

The rest of that province, of course, is the island of Newfoundland, with the world's most famous commercial fishing grounds, the beleaguered Grand Banks, lying seaward of its eastern tip. Famous Salmon waters rim virtually the entire island, and many of the streams boast good runs of Seatrout as well. Many of both species are also caught in the estuaries and "sea pools" of rivers. In addition, Newfoundland offers some big-game angling for Giant Bluefin Tuna, Shark, and an occasional Swordfish. Despite the depleted state of commercial offshore fisheries, recreational angling for Mackerel is productive all around the coast, while jigging and bait fishing for Cod and other groundfish remain good, at least for recreational purposes.

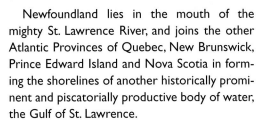

Newfoundland lies in the mouth of the mighty St. Lawrence River, and joins the other Atlantic Provinces of Quebec, New Brunswick, Prince Edward Island and Nova Scotia in forming the shorelines of another historically prominent and piscatorially productive body of water, the Gulf of St. Lawrence.

Although Atlantic Salmon rule the sportfishing roost along the entire rim of the Gulf, its saltwater menu also offers Tuna, Cod, Haddock, Hake and plenty of Mackerel. The latter fish even manages to lure quite a few fly rodders away from their diet of Salmon and Trout fishing.

Of all the Atlantic provinces, Nova Scotia, with shorelines fronting the Gulf of St. Lawrence, the Bay of Fundy and the Atlantic Ocean proper, probably ranks highest in terms of marine angling. Nova Scotia has long been famous for its Giant Bluefin Tuna, from Cape Breton Island in the north to Wedgeport in the south, and despite the management problems with this great fish in recent years, big Tuna are still available, though tightly regulated. Additionally, ports all along the East Coast are well stocked with boats that pursue Haddock, Cod, Pollock, Tautog, Flounder and Mackerel. Bonuses are annual runs of

Striped Bass and Bluefish. Stripers are most plentiful along the south-east and southern shores of Nova Scotia and in the Bay of Fundy.

MAINE

With nearly 3,500 miles of tidal shore, Maine boasts the most of any Atlantic state—more by a shade than North Carolina, Virginia or east-coast Florida. The coast is ragged, rocky and liberally dotted with coves and islands, making for a great variety of fishing situations. Happily, there is also a great variety of fish to fit the environment.

Striped Bass may top the prestige list among inshore fishermen, but are challenged in popularity by Bluefish, Mackerel, Pollock, Winter Flounder, Sand Dab, Tautog and even Cod and Haddock. The latter two tend to hang out near shore in the colder seasons, but the rest are mainly warm-weather targets, generally showing up in spring and stay-ing on the scene until late fall. Most of those fish are available to surf and shore fishermen as well as boating anglers.

Maine also is the only state with established runs of Atlantic Salmon, and it has not been too rare in the past to hear of an angler catching both Salmon and Striped Bass in some of the southeastern rivers. Note, though, that the Salmon fishery—as is the case nearly every-where—is subject to rigid regulation, even total closure at times, in coastal waters as well as the rivers.

Fishing for Bluefin Tuna is the chief big-game attraction out of Maine seaports, but there also is considerable interest in Shark fishing. The Blue Shark is the top species, but an occasional Mako is taken, along with some Porbeagle and Thresher. Partyboats berth at many spots along the coast and fish both inshore and offshore waters. Most spe-cialize in Cod, Haddock and Pollock, but some chase Stripers and Blues in season.

Many small-boat guides ply these waters, primarily for Stripers, Blues and Mackerel, and quite a few of the guides specialize in fly fishing.

Among Maine's many recreational ports are Eastport at the mouth of Cobscook Bay, Jonesport, Bar Harbor, Cranberry Isles and Isleford (Seal Harbor), North Haven at the mouth of Penobscot Bay, Thomaston, Boothbay, Kennebunkport and York Harbor.

NEW HAMPSHIRE

Although New Hampshire's coast is only 13 miles long, its tidal shoreline stretches to 131 miles and offers many more fishing opportunities than you might guess — thanks to a series of protected stream mouths, coves and beaches, dotted by rocky points. The compact package is even more appealing when you consider that all the spots are easily accessible off U. S. 1, the coastal highway. And I-95 runs only about a mile inland.

For anglers seeking a workout, Bluefin Tuna are often to be found only a couple of miles offshore from Portsmouth, around the Isles of Shoals. Hampton and Seabrook are other jump-off spots.

In addition to Tuna, hefty Pollock are top draws for the deepwater crowd, while small Pollock offer light-tackle fun in the Piscataqua River mouth, and around Newcastle and Great Bay near Portsmouth. Both offshore and inshore, Cod and Haddock add to the bag, along with Cusk and Hake.

In coastal waters, the leading attraction — as easily guessed — is the Striped Bass. Small school bass often provide dependable action, and lunker catches are increasing steadily. The Piscataqua, again, is a good bet for Stripers, especially below Portsmouth and at Dover Point. Hampton Harbor is another prime area. Again, light-tackle casters make hay with both school Stripers and Mackerel. Tautog also get a lot of attention here.

Fishing piers and docks dot the compact coast of New Hampshire, adding more access for shorebound anglers, who also cast from beaches and points.

Partyboats and charterboats, along with small-boat rentals and private facilities, are liberally spaced along the beach highway at Wallis Sands, Rye Beach, Little Boars Head, Great Boars Head, Hampton Beach and Seabrook Beach near the Massachusetts state line.

MASSACHUSETTS

Cape Cod is the showplace area of Massachusetts sport fishing, and its big star, once more, is the Striped Bass. The Cape's outer beaches are paradise for the surf fisherman, while boaters chase their

Stripers—along with Bluefish and other popular types—not only in the Atlantic proper, but also in Nantucket Sound to the south of the Cape, and in Cape Cod Bay and Buzzards Bay to the west and southwest. The Cape Cod Canal connects the latter two bodies and is itself a famous producer of Striped Bass for shoreside anglers, especially at night. Striper fishing begins in late spring in all areas and continues through fall.

The Cape's entire outside shore, from the tip of Monomoy Island on the south end to Race Point on the north, is a stomping ground for Stripers, and there are regular access points for surf fishermen. Jetties offer additional good spots from which to fling baits for Stripers and Blues, while boaters also work the beaches just outside the breakers.

Guides for surf fishermen, along with beach buggies, are available on the Cape. Angling facilities and launching ramps are plentiful in all areas. Both charter and private boaters often mix Little Tunny, Atlantic Bonito and even Spanish Mackerel with Stripers and Blues.

Charterboats of various sizes and prices also work offshore waters, where Bluefin Tuna are the biggest prizes, along with Sharks of several species. Cod are the principal bottom targets, although other tasty fish, of course, swim with them. In summer, various migratory fish from the South might appear offshore at uncertain times—even an occasional Dolphin or Marlin. Charters, both inshore and offshore, work out of Chatham, Dennis, Hyannis, Orleans, Barnstable, Harwichport and scattered other locations.

The islands of Martha's Vineyard and Nantucket, south of Cape Cod, feed from the same fishy menu as already described—from surf to offshore. For boaters, the roaring rip east of Nantucket is one of the most famous, and most dependable, spots to tangle with big Bluefish and bass of all sizes, including some monsters.

Another island rich in local angling lore is Cuttyhunk, the seaward extension of the Elizabeth Islands, which form the southern boundary of Buzzards Bay. Big bass and Bluefish prowl the shores and rips of the area, while Buzzard's Bay itself is home to great quantities of school-size Bass and occasionally hosts schools of Bonito. Bluefish, Flounder, Tautog and Weakfish also are caught in the bay.

Despite the richly deserved reputation of Cape Cod and the islands, saltwater angling prospects do not diminish much, if any, as you work north of Cape Cod. Plymouth and Plymouth Bay offer good fishing in the summer for Stripers, along with Bluefish, Pollock, Mackerel and others. And Boston Harbor itself is sometimes aboil with schooling Stripers. Big bass aren't usually plentiful in the harbor, but are not exactly rare, either. Boston-area anglers also take Flounder, small Cod and a variety of other bottom fish in the bay, while bigger Cod, Haddock and Pollock await farther offshore.

From Boston Harbor to Cape Ann, and around to Plum Island in the far north of the state, there are quite a few good surf-fishing areas. Gloucester, historically famous as a commercial fishing center, now is a kickoff point for some of New England's best Bluefin Tuna angling and groundfishing — although the Tuna fishery, as everywhere, experiences sharp ups and downs. Charters, ramps and full angling facilities are well stocked around several ports, including Gloucester, Cape Ann and Rockport.

Among the storied offshore destinations of the area are Cashes Ledge, an underwater mountain about 80 miles out from Gloucester, and two famous offshore banks: Stellwagon Bank, running between Cape Ann and Cape Cod, some 25 miles east of Boston; and Georges Bank about 120 miles southeast of Gloucester, which covers 1,000 square miles or so and offers probably the best Codfishing in New England. Those and many closer spots produce numerous different bottom species, as well as Bluefin and other Tunas in season. Dolphin and billfish can add to the fun in summer.

RHODE ISLAND

It may be the smallest state, but Rhode Island stands tall in saltwater fishing opportunities. From spring through fall, Striped Bass generally are in good supply all along the coast and inside the bays and estuaries. And some very big Bass still are taken each year.

Narragansett Bay, often referred to as New England's best "fish trap," begins loading up with Stripers in April or May. The smaller fish prefer to roam the rivers and flats, while the bigger boys stick mostly to the points and islands around the entrance to the bay. Both boaters and surfcasters take good fish from Sakonnet Point on the eastern flank to Point Judith at the bay's western end — and at numerous spots in between, including (but certainly not limited to) Saschuet point, Easton Point, Beavertail Point and Sakonnet Point. And those outside spots only begin to scratch the many fishy offerings to be found inside Narragansett Bay.

West of the bay, from Point Judith to the Connecticut border at the Pawcatuck River, the Striped Bass may start romping even earlier in the season. In that sector, the top areas include Watch Hill, Weekapaug and Quonchontaug. Big bass are taken with fair regularity at Charlestown Beach and in the Charlestown Breachway, between Quonchontaug and Point Judith. Anglers in all the areas mentioned also rely on Bluefish to provide a good share of the action.

Off Rhode Island's coast lies another truly historic fishing center, Block Island.

Big game is much in the picture here, especially Bluefin Tuna and White Marlin. Only a vestige is left, however, of the Swordfishing that once drew attention to the island. (Of course, the Swordfish decline, brought about by merciless commercial longlining, is worldwide.) Surf and inshore fishermen also love Block Island. Throughout the spring-to-fall season it can be depended on to produce some of the best action on Striped Bass and Bluefish in the state. Rhode Islanders are not the only anglers who take regular advantage of Block Island's bounty. Ferries run to Block Island from New London, Connecticut, and several terminals on Long Island, New York, as well as from Rhode Island ports.

The big-game species mentioned are fished out of the mainland, as well as from Block Island, and all areas of Rhode Island have seasonal access — usually in late summer or early fall — to schools of Atlantic Bonito and Little Tunny (False Albacore), along with school Bluefin Tuna and a few giant Bluefins.

For the less adventurous, Rhode Island's inshore waters offer a fine variety of other favorite species, including Weakfish, Pollock, Scup, Fluke, Flounder and Tautog.

CONNECTICUT

Although lunkers have always been in pretty scarce supply, few areas of the Atlantic Coast can match Connecticut's output of action on school-size Striped Bass. Moreover, the season gets started earlier than in most places, with fish sometimes beginning to show up in the rivers, starting in the Thames and Connecticut rivers, as early as February. Both the fishermen and the bass, however, generally prefer to wait until April. By early summer, the fish have migrated all along the Connecticut coast.

Good early action for school Stripers, either by casting or trolling, is usually to be found in the estuaries in April. The lower Connecticut River around Saybrook Point is prime territory, as are New London's Niantic estuary, the Thames River estuary, Greenwich-Cos Cob Harbor and the mouth of the Housatonic River. As the weather warms, action increases around the Fish Islands off Darien, the Norwalk Islands off Norwalk, and Fishers Island off New London. Fisher's Island Sound is a fine fishing ground for anglers out of Mystic, Groton, Long Point and Mason Island.

Not surprisingly, all the areas enumerated as Striper territory are really all-around producers of many other species, including lots of Bluefish, Porgies (Scup), Fluke, Pollock, Weakfish and Blackfish (Tautog).

In early fall, Atlantic Bonito and Little Tunny join the menu, both off the coastline and inside some estuaries, such as Niantic Bay.

There are many seashore communities all along the Connecticut coast that offer facilities for angling and boating, along with charter boats and skiff guides for trolling, casting or fly fishing. Some Connecticut charterboats, most of them from around New London and Stonington, travel to Block Island in quest of Bluefin Tuna.

NEW YORK

Basically, New York saltwater angling means Long Island saltwater angling. But there are a few exceptions and the major one is in the lower Hudson River — New York Harbor itself. Numerous species of fish both glamorous and pedestrian are targets of angling activity in the harbor, but by far the most important is Striped Bass, which begins an annual run in late March or April. Much of this fishing is conducted in historic settings indeed, with the Statue of Liberty, Ellis Island and the

Manhattan skyline as backdrops.

Many boating trips originate, and much shore fishing takes place, across the Hudson in New Jersey. One of the most popular spots is Liberty State Park in Jersey City, where both a launching ramp and fine shore casting opportunities are found. Regardless of which side of the river you kick off from, the entire Harbor is New York water.

Sportsmen in the metropolitan area are not limited to a diet of Striped Bass. Quite a few varieties of fish are caught from various shoreline spots and aboard both private and fish-for-pay vessels. Boating anglers work both the harbor and south of it in the New York Bight and off the Jersey coast. Their take includes Bluefish, Weakfish, Flounder, Porgy and Tautog, and they are harassed by the usual pests, such as Sea Robins.

Long Island, though, is the promised land of New York coastal fishing. It has everything, and if considerable travel is often required, the facilities are up to it. Good rail service and an interstate highway run the length of the island from New York City to Montauk on the east end — a distance of more than 100 miles.

Rental and charterboats plus an array of private facilities await the angler on the south shore at (west to east) such locations as Coney Island, the Rockaways, Freeport, Jones Inlet, Fire Island, Patchogue, Hampton Bays, Amagansett and Montauk.

On the north side, anglers fish in Long Island Sound out of Oyster Bay, Cold Spring Harbor, North Port, Port Jefferson and a string of other communities eastward to Orient Point.

Montauk, of course, not only deserves its rank as the "capital" of New York sport fishing, but also rates as one of the premier angling centers of the whole Atlantic Coast, providing many top-drawer opportunities both inshore and offshore. Striped Bass lead the coastal list of targets, with Bluefish close behind. Good shore fishing spots abound from beaches, jetties and rocks, while anglers who prefer boats have a huge variety of party and charter craft to choose from. Offshore, the major drawing cards are sharks of several kinds — Blues, Makos and Threshers being prominent — and Bluefin Tuna of various sizes up to huge. Yellowfin Tuna are sometimes numerous as well. In summer, billfish join the fun. These are mostly White Marlin, with an occasional Blue Marlin and an even more occasional Swordfish taking the baits. Smaller ocean gamefish, such as Bonito, Little Tunny and Mackerel also are at hand.

Partyboats out of eastern and northern Long Island rely most of the time on such fare as Stripers, Blues, Flounder, Sea Bass, Weakfish and Porgy, but in the colder months they switch to seeking Cod, Haddock and other groundfish.

The south shore of Long Island is a surf fisherman's paradise, with many fine beaches spotted along the entire length of that coast. Atlantic Beach, Long Beach, Fire Island Inlet, Great South Bay, Shinnecock Inlet and Montauk are the best known.

NEW JERSEY

From Sandy Hook south to Cape May, New Jersey offers the saltwater angler well over 120 miles of Atlantic coastline—much of it outstanding territory for surfcasters, jetty fishermen and other shorebound anglers. But that's only the barest of beginnings. Offshore of that coast, an outstanding mix of both cold and warm water gamefish awaits the seagoing angler, while inside stretches a huge array of protected waterways. Inlets, river mouths and bays are dotted along the entire coast, some of the best known being Barnegat Bay, Great Bay, Egg Harbor and Absecon but there are numerous others.

The potential bag list of inshore game species—whether fishing from surf, jetty, or boat—includes Blues, Stripers, Red Drum, Weakfish, Flounder, Croaker and Kingfish (Whiting). Prime surfcasting begins on the north shore and continues past Sandy Hook to cover virtually every sector of the coast.

Charter and partyboats berth at nearly every Atlantic coast community, starting at Sandy Hook, with other major fleets sailing out of Hoboken, Atlantic Beach, Atlantic Highlands, Sea Bright, Monmouth Beach, Neptune, Brielle, Point Pleasant, Island Beach, Tom's Harbor, Barnegat Light, Atlantic City, Ocean City, Avalon and Wildwood— among others. No shortage of fishing boats in this state!

Bluefish, along with Striped Bass, have historically been the backbone of Jersey charter fishing. Both chumming and trolling are widely practiced for Bluefish in nearshore waters, while Stripers generally are sought by trolling, either along the jetties or outside the surf. Schooling tuna, including Albacore and Bluefins, some giants, are often fairly close at hand too, in summer and early fall.

The more adventurous charters head much farther offshore, where the potential bag increases accordingly, in both variety and size. The offshore dropoffs and canyon depths hold big Bluefin and Yellowfin Tuna, White Marlin and a few Blue Marlin, along with Albacore and even Dolphin.

Partyboats rely heavily on Porgy, Flounder, Sea Bass and Tautog, along with Croaker, Spot and, of course, Bluefish, when they are available. Cold weather partyboat trips look to Cod and Pollock for action.

New Jersey's fine fishing does not end at Cape May but continues into Delaware Bay, where the menu includes Weakfish (and Spotted Seatrout too), along with Bluefish, Croaker, Flounder and an assortment of small stuff. Boats and angling facilities are well distributed on that shore, as well, with a few of the top locations being Bivalve, Fortescue, Greenwich and Reeds Beach.

Rivers flowing into the Jersey side of the Bay—such as the Shrewsbury and Navesink—often turn up fast action for small Bluefish in summer.

DELAWARE

Although its coastline is barely more than 25 miles long, Delaware crams plenty of saltwater fishing punch into this small package, with good prospects to be found in the Atlantic and in Rehoboth and Delaware bays.

Surf fishing is good at various spots on the Atlantic shore from Cape Henlopen in the north to Fenwick Island near the Maryland border. And also from some beaches in the lower Delaware Bay, from Cape Henlopen to about Bowers Beach.

Private boating facilities and many charter and partyboats are packed into Delaware's fishy southeast section, with the biggest fleets located just inside Cape Henlopen at Lewes, and around Rehoboth Beach and the Indian River Inlet. Other trips into the Atlantic start from Delaware Bay marinas and ramps, up to about Bowers Beach.

In the summer season, anglers generally concentrate on Bluefish, Weakfish, Kingfish and Croaker, plus an assortment of bottom feeders that includes Tautog, Sea Bass and Flounder. Black Drum and Red Drum also join the fun in warm weather.

White Marlin and a few Blue Marlin draw the top attention from offshore fishermen, who also take Dolphin, Bonito, False Albacore and school Bluefin Tuna. Bottom fishing outside produces some Cod as well as Porgy, Sea Bass and Flounder.

The northern shore of Delaware Bay fronts shallow water in many areas and is good ground for Croaker, Porgy, Flounder, Weakfish and Tautog. Bluefish also stage summer runs. Jumpoff spots with good facilities are at New Castle, Delaware Beach, the mouth of the Chesapeake and Delaware Canal, Port Penn, Bay View and Woodland Beach, which marks the area where the river widens into the lower bay.

MARYLAND

Saltwater fishing in Maryland splits into two major components — each of them ranking among the best on the East Coast. One is ocean fishing off the state's Eastern Shore; the other, inside fishing in Chesapeake Bay. This great bay, shared, of course, with Virginia, itself seems of oceanesque proportions to boating anglers, both in area and varied fish population.

Although there is no doubt that the Striped Bass — locally called Rockfish, or, simply, "Rock" — is the biggest sporting pet, it only begins a long list of Chesapeake Bay offerings. Stripers are found throughout the bay, from the Susquehanna River above Baltimore all the way to the ocean shores. Various saltwater gamesters routinely travel far up the bay as well, but the closer one gets to the bay's vast mouth, the better the saltwater fishing becomes. Striped Bass, again, might be found anywhere, but in the lower regions they yield some of their popularity to Cobia, Red Drum, Bluefish, Black Drum, Croaker and a vast array of willing biters with less prestige.

Both Stripers and Shad stage runs of various size in most streams of the Chesapeake, including the Potomac River, where they at times run all the way to the vicinity of Washington D.C. Other productive rivers convenient to anglers from Washington and Baltimore include the Magothy, just below Baltimore, the Severn with the city of Annapolis at its mouth, and the South River.

Another great river of the western shore is the Patuxent. Fine facilities in that sector are to be found at California, Benedict and Solomons. The latter is an especially popular starting spot, with a full array of facilities. Like many other Chesapeake rivers, the area of the Patuxent offers a heady mix of salt and freshwater prospects, headed (as usual) by Stripers in season, but also including Seatrout, Flounder, White Perch, Bluefish and Spot. Incidentally, White Perch rank as potential prey for youngsters from virtually every dock and shoreline in Chesapeake Bay.

Again, there is much fishing in the bay, especially in the lower regions, that is not directly associated with the famous rivers. The Chesapeake is a huge spawning ground and contains so many species that the angler can almost always bend his rod on something, whether he hits his target or not. Boats — private, charter and party — take to the bay from every port along the shore. To name just a few: Deale, Fairhaven, Holland Point, North Beach and Chesapeake Beach. Top seasons are summer and fall.

On Maryland's Eastern Shore, there is good surf fishing around Ocean City and on Assateague Island, which is reached by boat or ferry. On those beaches, Striped Bass are joined in spring and fall by big Red Drum. Smaller prey includes Bluefish, Kingfish and a few Seatrout. On the inside of Assateague Island, small-boat fishermen find Bluefish, Seatrout, Porgy, Sea Bass and Flounder.

As for offshore angling, Ocean City is one of the busiest sportfishing ports in the Mid-Atlantic. And it is world famous for its White Marlin in an area about 23 miles offshore, known as the "Jack Spot." But the Whites are not alone. Ocean trollers consistently take good mixed bags that include everything from Blue Marlin and tuna (both Bluefin and Yellowfin) to Dolphin, Wahoo, Bonito and Albacore. In fall and winter, some charterboats offer bottom-fishing outings for Cod. Headboats, however, mostly stick fairly close to shore, concentrating on such fare as Porgy and Sea Bass.

VIRGINIA

Just as in Maryland, Striped Bass or "Rockfish" hog most of the angling conversation among Virginia's bay fishermen; however, the lower reaches of Chesapeake Bay are a paradise for potluck anglers as well, offering an abundance of sport species, large and small. Among many others, these include Bluefish, Cobia, Red and Black Drum, Croaker, Flounder, Weakfish, Whiting, Porgy and Sea Bass.

Shad also provide an important fishery in the spring — mostly, of course, in the rivers entering the bay. Striper fishing begins in spring, peaks in early summer, and then enjoys another peak in the fall. Although bass are commonly taken up the rivers, it is the flats fishing out in the bay that turns on the huge majority of anglers. The fish aren't often of great size but can provide sizzling action for casters, trollers and bait fishermen alike.

Much of this action takes place in the area known as the "Northern Neck," between the Potomac and Rappahannock Rivers, where charters and other fine facilities are available at Weems, Whitestone, Irvington, and, farther north, Reedsville, Coles Point and Colonial Beach up the Potomac. Partyboats chase Stripers and other fish out of many of those landings. Other prime jump-off spots can be found on the neck of land between the Rappahannock and the York rivers at a number of communities, including Urbanna and Deltaville.

Windmill Point at the Rappahannock's mouth is a center for Cobia fishing from the middle of summer into late fall. Anglers concentrate on the area around Rappahannock Light and usually chum for their Cobia. Other charters and services are found at Deltaville, Kilmarnock and Irvington.

The offshore islands of Virginia's Atlantic shore — the most prominent being Chincoteague, Wachapreague and Cobb — are among the most famous and productive grounds on the whole coast for surfcasters. Peak activity is in the summer and the menu is impressive indeed — headed up by huge Red and Black Drum, Striped Bass and Bluefish. Flounder, Whiting and other smaller varieties also abound. All the species travel sloughs fairly close to shore, or even very close in some areas, and so there is a place for light casting tackle as well as traditional surf gear. More and similar opportunities are to be found across the mouth of the bay on the southern end of the Delmarva Peninsula, at Cape Charles and other communities.

Charterboats along Virginia's outer coast vary a great deal in size and price, since the fleets go after everything from Blue Marlin, White Marlin and Dolphin far offshore, to Red Drum and Striped Bass in the inshore waters and sounds.

Partyboats are available, too, along with marina facilities, at Quinby, Wachapreague, Chincoteague and other ports along the coast.

NORTH CAROLINA

A double jolt of helpful geography makes North Carolina a pivotal point of the Atlantic Coast fishery, and one with an unusual wealth of finny resources. For one thing it is centrally located and, therefore, collects a bounty of both coldwater and warmwater sport species. For the other, its seaward extension brings it closer to the deep blue ocean at the edge of the continental shelf than most other Atlantic Coast areas. Adding more spice is the fact that the Gulf Stream and the Labrador Current meet at Diamond Shoals off Cape Hatteras.

Boats sailing from various ports along the coast reap a bluewater harvest headed by the largest Blue Marlin of U.S. waters — along with smaller Blues, plenty of White Marlin and quite a few Sailfish. As to fish without beaks, outstanding results on giant Bluefin Tuna are recorded each year, and in all seasons except winter, there seems always to be a grab bag available that might include Yellowfin and school Bluefin Tuna, plus Dolphin, Wahoo and Skipjack.

Closer inshore, around shoals and wrecks, much of the attention switches to King Mackerel, Amberjack, Cobia, Barracuda, Grouper, Snapper and assorted smaller fish. And North Carolina offers ample partyboats and private marina facilities to go after them.

Charter fleets are located at Nags Head, Hatteras, Oregon Inlet, Morehead City and — in the southern end of the state near Wilmington — Southport, Wrightsville Beach and Carolina Beach. But that only begins a long list. Basically, any port with access to the sea offers boating and angling facilities.

Much of the North Carolina coast is enclosed by the Outer Banks, which extend roughly from Portsmouth Island in the north to Cape Lookout. The Outer Banks is a long strip of sandy islands, whose contribution to the sportfishing picture is manifold. To start with, the outer beaches are probably the most productive — and certainly the most famous — surf fishing grounds on the South Atlantic Coast. They attract, mostly in the fall, huge Red Drum that commonly top 50 pounds and sometimes push 100 pounds. But many other sport species roam the surf as well, including Striped Bass, Bluefish, Black Drum and Spotted Seatrout along with Whiting, Croaker, Spot and various "pest" species.

Fishermen not caught up in the surf mystique get to sample that same fishy menu from numerous fishing piers that dot the coast. In addition, pier anglers also get shots at Tarpon, King and Spanish Mackerel, Cobia and some other pelagic species that rarely are taken by surfers.

In addition to beachfront fishing, the Outer Banks are important because of the inlets between the islands that help "trade" gamefish between the ocean and the chain of protected sounds — Pamlico, Croatan, Roanoke and Albemarle — that lie inside them. Spotted Seatrout and small Red Drum ("Puppy Drum") may grab the most angling attention, but the sounds turn out a huge variety that includes big Red and Black Drum, Striped Bass and Cobia.

Among many ports offering guides and facilities for protected water angling are Manns Harbor on the mainland, Manteo and Wanchese on Roanoke Island, and Ocracoke on the Outer Banks. Near Morehead City, marinas are located at Harkers Island, Atlantic and Cedar Island, among other communities. South of the sounds, good fishing continues in the narrower Intracoastal Waterway to Wilmington and Cape Fear, out of such landings as Morehead City, Swansboro, Folkstone, Wrightsville Beach, Carolina Beach, Southport and Shallotte.

SOUTH CAROLINA

Salty angling opportunities are many in South Carolina, ranging from fine fishing in protected waters for Seatrout, Redfish and other favorites, to productive surf fishing, to action-packed offshore trolling and bottom fishing. It is in South Carolina, incidentally, that "Red Drum" start to become "Redfish"—a name that continues through Georgia and Florida and around the entire Gulf Coast.

Much of South Carolina's fishing activity clusters around Myrtle Beach, Ocean Drive Beach, Little River and Georgetown on the northern half of the coast. It is not quite so far from those ports out to deep blue water as it is in the south, and charterboats making the long trip frequently connect with Blue and White Marlin, Tuna and Sailfish. However, the lion's share of attention—by charterboats, partyboats and private craft alike—is devoted to gamesters that romp much closer to shore. There are quite a few of these, but none quite so popular, in season, as the King Mackerel.

In addition to Kings, partyboats and private craft do well on Spanish Mackerel, Cobia, Amberjack, Barracuda and Little Tunny, along with Grouper, Snapper, Sea Bass, Porgy and other bottom favorites.

U.S. 17 runs the length of the South Carolina coast and you seldom travel far along that artery before hitting another location that offers charterboats, partyboats or private boating facilities.

The inshore fishing starts, as you might guess, right on many Carolina beaches, where surfers successfully seek Red Drum, Bluefish, Black Drum and a host of smaller favorites, including Spot and Whiting. Angling in bays and sounds provides regular action on a variety of fish, large and small, headed by Seatrout, small Redfish and Sheepshead. As for big Reds, the jetty at Georgetown is a famous spot, as is Bull Island near Cape Romain.

Small-boat fishing is productive in all areas of Charleston's harbor, with catches ranging from Trout and Drum to Sheepshead, Flounder and, in fact, the entire menu of inshore species. Good pier and bridge fishing is also handy throughout this area for the same lineup. Offshore trips for both trolling and bottom fishing are offered at various docks in the harbor.

Although it has to compete with many other attractions, the best fishing on the southern end of the coast is around Hilton Head, a large resort island just north of the Georgia border. Good boating facilities are offered there, including guided inshore and outside fishing. A fine network of protected water holds Red Drum, Seatrout, Flounder, Sheepshead and others, while the outside trolling produces, in season, King Mackerel and Cobia, plus bottom fish.

GEORGIA

The Peach State packs plenty of saltwater action into a short coastline of only 100 miles. That's possible because the modest total goes up by more than 23 times after you add on the tidal shorelines of all the islands, inlets, bays and estuaries that blanket the coast from the Savannah River on the northern border to the St. Marys River at the Florida state line.

Savannah, Brunswick and St. Marys are the principal fishing ports, but boating facilities, guides, charters and shore fishing are well dispersed along most of the coast, especially around Darien, Crescent, and many places on Sea Island, St. Simons Island, Jekyll Island (all near Brunswick) and Tybee Island near Savannah.

As in South Carolina (and northern Florida), King Mackerel stage big annual rallies off the Georgia coast and are the favorite target of offshore fishermen, especially the private small-boat fleet; however, charterboats — mostly out of Savannah, Brunswick and St. Marys — do get out to the Gulf Stream. There they find Sailfish and an occasional Marlin, along with Dolphin, Barracuda, Amberjack, small types of Tuna and a few others. Partyboats and bottom fishermen add Grouper, Red Snapper, Porgy and Sea Bass.

Closer to the beaches, Spanish Mackerel, huge Jack Crevalle, Cobia and even Tarpon help keep boaters happy. The Tarpon appear in spring and stay around through the warm months. Most are hooked around the inlets or along the outside beaches, but some come into the Georgia river mouths.

From the ocean beaches, notably around the inlets, surf fishermen take some fat Redfish that sometimes top 40 pounds. They also get Bluefish in twice-yearly runs and the usual assortment of surf bottom feeders.

The menu inside the sounds and other protected waters features Seatrout of both the spotted and gray varieties, Redfish, Sheepshead, Black Drum and Flounder.

Georgia is just about the southernmost romping grounds of Striped Bass. Stripers do make it as far as Florida's St. Johns River, but in Georgia they can be taken in the surf and inlets and in bays and sounds, as well as several rivers. Shad, too, come into the estuaries and rivers, notably the Savannah, Altamaha, Ogeechee and St. Marys (shared with Florida). Striped Bass generally show up in the spring, while Shad normally make their appearance shortly after the first of the year, staying until perhaps April.

FLORIDA

Florida's Atlantic Coast undergoes a change of piscatorial character around Cape Canaveral. From the Cape north to Georgia, the angling menu includes many temperate species and the prospects are quite similar to those of the South Carolina and Georgia coasts. An ever-increasing mix of subropical species, however, does add a great deal of spice to North Florida fishing. South of the Cape, considerably warmer water makes for a bigger variety and, for certain species, longer fishing seasons. One major reason for this is because the edge of the continental shelf, with its bordering Gulf Stream current, begins turning closer to shore, reaching the nearest point off the Palm Beaches and remaining very close through the rest of South Florida and the Keys.

Regardless, though, extended periods of warm weather — common in recent years — are likely to scramble the temperature barriers and send "tropical" species, such as Snook, wandering far north of their typical range, even as far as the Jacksonville area.

The Cape Canaveral "dividing line" does have a heavy impact on offshore fishing, but not so much in quality or variety as in travel time. Boats out of Fernandina Beach, Jacksonville, St. Augustine, Daytona and the Cape Canaveral area typically head seaward a dozen miles, or even much more, before tossing over lines to troll for Sailfish, Dolphin and other bluewater gamefish. The necessary distance is noticeably reduced for anglers out of Sebastian, Vero Beach and Fort Pierce. It shrinks even shorter off Stuart, and comes close to fading away altogether off the Palm Beaches, where blue water almost kisses the surf. Boats out of Greater Fort Lauderdale, Greater Miami and most of the Keys have just a short run to Gulf Stream grounds.

Still, the offshore menu never changes much over the whole coast, although seasonal abundance does. Sailfish are the most prestigious prize, simply because there are so many more of them than Blue and White Marlin. North Floridians get most of their Sails in the summer;

South Florida anglers during the cool months, when Sails often invade in incredible numbers.

While Sails get the publicity, other species — especially Dolphin and King Mackerel — provide the most action for the most fishermen. They are joined by Spanish and Cero Mackerel, Wahoo, Little Tunny (called Bonito in Florida), Skipjack Tuna and, on occasion, some big Yellowfin Tuna.

Partyboats and private bottom fishermen also find much the same fare in both North and South Florida, with Grouper and Snapper being the most-sought prizes, along with Amberjack, Porgies, Yellowtail, Grunts and, especially in the South, a huge variety of reef species as well.

Close to shore and inside, Tarpon, Redfish and Trout are the big draws, joined by Snook from roughly Cape Canaveral southward. The world's biggest Spotted Seatrout roam Central Florida lagoons, primarily the Indian River, and Redfish in those same waters also run much larger than the Florida average.

Other shallow-water favorites of the entire Florida Atlantic Coast include Pompano, Permit, Black Drum, Jack Crevalle of all sizes to more than 50 pounds, Sheepshead, Tripletail and Flounder (mostly Central and North).

From Miami's Biscayne Bay through the Keys, sight fishing for Bonefish, Permit, Tarpon and a few other gamesters grabs a huge chunk of attention from both residents and visiting anglers. Major fishing locations in the Keys are, east to west (most folks tend to think of it as north to south) Key Largo, Islamorada, Marathon and Key West. However, there are literally dozens of other locations throughout the Keys that offer guides, charters, and top-flight angling and boating facilities.

How to Use This Book

Surprisingly, many of the fish that are commonly taken along the Atlantic Coast are familiar to anglers in both southern and northern waters. Striped Bass and Bluefish are only the most prominent of quite a few nearshore species that ramble, in their appropriate seasons, over much of the Atlantic coastline. Out in deeper water, various Tunas and other offshore gamesters bend rods from Florida to Nova Scotia.

Most species, however, are confined to limited geographic ranges by temperature, bottom conditions, or other biological and environmental factors. This means, of course, that anglers who are reasonably familiar with the common sport fish in their usual stomping grounds are pretty sure to encounter a bewildering array of new species when they travel to another area of the Atlantic Coast — as so many devoted sportsmen are able to do these days.

But, regardless of whether they work home waters or vacation waters, or whether they chase migratory or resident species, all Atlantic Coast anglers can be sure of one thing: There are so many different kinds of fish out there that anyone who fishes regularly is certain to encounter numerous unfamiliar types. Additional problems often arise in attempting to distinguish certain species from others in the same family; for instance, Mackerels, Croakers, Flounders or Snappers, to name just a few of the bigger groups.

Up until now, the angler has had little published help in sorting out his potential catch. The available reference books have generally fallen into one of two categories — those that cover only a relatively few well-known sport species, or else more scientific volumes that blanket nearly everything with fins, leaving it up to the poor fisherman to dig what he's looking for out of a bewildering array of fishes, many of which he is never likely to encounter and many more that are of no interest at all to the sportsman.

This book is different. It is designed strictly for the recreational fisherman and is aimed at describing and illustrating virtually every species an angler is likely to find on the end of his line anywhere on the Atlantic Coast — in deep water or shallow and from the Canadian Maritime Provinces to the Florida Keys.

Yes, they're all here — some 250 of them — panfish, prestigious game fish and irritating pests alike. Even the most popular and productive bait species are included.

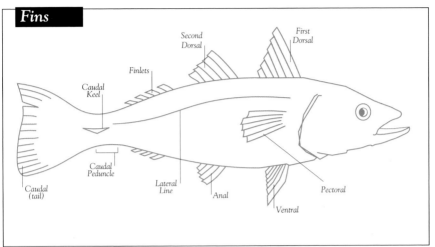

Fins

First Dorsal

Second Dorsal

Finlets

Caudal Keel

Caudal Peduncle

Caudal (tail)

Lateral Line

Anal

Ventral

Pectoral

Here's a typical configuration of fins useful for identification.

And, more than just a guide to identification, the book provides essential basic information concerning where and how to go after them, and how each species rates in fighting ability and table quality.

It would be nice if all the fish in the book could be sorted into neat chapters according to habitat. Then the offshore angler could find all his potential catches in one section and the flats fisherman could turn to another. Sadly, though, such a neat arrangement cannot work well, because the majority of covered species are at home in a variety of water depths and environments. Cod, for instance, are mostly taken far offshore, but they inhabit close-in areas as well, and are even fair game for surf fishermen in certain places and seasons. To cite a similar example from more southerly waters, Red Drum are common catches in the open sea, on the beach, over shallow protected flats, and in freshwater rivers. Even pelagic gamesters like Little Tunny, King Mackerel and Sailfish are fair game at many Atlantic piers.

For lack of any more logical arrangement, most chapters in the book cover a single family of fishes. This makes for handy identification because related types almost always share certain common characteristics. A number of our most popular sport fish, however, do not belong to large families at all, but are either the lone member of a particular family or else the only one of keen interest to sport fishermen. Those fish share a chapter entitled "Rugged Individuals."

THE INDIVIDUAL ENTRIES

For ease of reference, the entry for every fish in the book is broken down into categories that answer the most common questions asked by fishermen about their catch. Each entry is headed by the most widely used common name, along with the scientific name and, of course, the color illustration. Because common names are anything but consistent, the scientific name is the only truly correct label. Other information is given as follows:

DESCRIPTION: Since individuals of any species can vary from the typical coloration and markings, it is important to consult both the illustration and the written description to assure positive identification.

OTHER NAMES: Some of the more popular common names used in different regions.

RANGE: The range in which the species is commonly found within the area covered by the book. Note that many fish have far wider ranges which may cover several countries, or even, in some cases, most of the world.

HABITAT: Tells where the adult fish are most likely to be found and hooked by anglers.

SIZE: Describes the usual size range of specimens taken by sportsmen. In most cases, estimates of the potential maximum size are also included.

FOOD VALUE: The table quality of a particular fish is highly subjective. The information here is based on established culinary reputation and on the author's personal opinion.

GAME QUALITIES: Again, this is based on the author's long personal experience and on extensive consultation with other anglers.

TACKLE AND BAITS: Recommends the most suitable types of tackle for both efficiency and good sport, plus a few standard or especially effective baits and lures. Experienced anglers will realize, however, that there is plenty of room for other choices.

FISHING SYSTEMS: Suggested techniques are defined as follows: Still Fishing (fishing with natural bait from a fixed position, ashore or afloat); Trolling (pulling artificial or natural baits behind a moving boat under propulsion); Drift Fishing (trailing natural baits or certain artificial lures behind a boat that is being moved by wind or current); Casting (manually casting and retrieving artificial lures with Spinning, Baitcasting, Surf or Fly outfits, either blindly or with sighted fish as targets).

FISHERY MANAGEMENT AND LAWS

Unfortunately, more than a few of the most popular hook-and-line species all along the Atlantic Coast (and throughout the world), now are experiencing an assortment of pressures — the heaviest being commercial overfishing — that threaten their overall numbers and even, in a few cases, their very existence.

But there is good news too. Rigid fishery management practices have been put in place by every state on the Atlantic Coast, as well as by the U.S. and Canadian governments. As a result, some troubled species are discernibly on the upswing, while the steady depletion of some others has been slowed drastically, if not yet eliminated.

All this has led to a sometimes highly confusing assortment of laws, compounded by the fact that these laws — permitting and catch limits in particular — often vary a great deal from region to region and from state to state. Because so many jurisdictions are involved, and because the rules are constantly being revised, it is impractical to go into detail here. Suffice it to say that an important part of any angler's homework these days is to be fully aware of the laws and to carefully observe all legal requirements. Happily, the huge majority of sportsmen these days are not only abiding by the law but going the extra mile by releasing many of their fish, whether legally required or not.

Mention inshore sportfishing along nearly the entire Atlantic Coast and one species will immediately pop to mind—the Striped Bass. Stripers not only are familiar to anglers from Nova Scotia all the way to Florida, but are rated as the No. 1 prize for most of them. This is especially so for anglers working the waters of New England, New York, New Jersey and the Mid-Atlantic states. Not that it matters a great deal, but only two other members of this family are ever likely to show up on the end of a line. One is the White Perch, which makes up in availability and cooperation what it lacks in size, and the other is the rare Wreckfish. Although the Black Sea Bass is very well known and as widely distributed as the Striper, it actually belongs to a different family—the Groupers (Chapter 14).

The Sea Basses

Striped Bass

White Perch

Wreckfish

Striped Bass

Morone saxatilis

OTHER NAMES:

Striper
Rock Bass
Rockfish

RANGE: *Most of the Atlantic Coast from Nova Scotia to North Florida. Prime range extends from Maine to the Carolinas.*

HABITAT: *Although a surf target of legendary stature, the Striped Bass is widespread along the coast and in bays and rivers, as well as in rips and over reefs not too far offshore. Bass like rocky areas, rough water and good current. Smaller fish, and occasional big ones, roam shallow flats feeding on schooling baitfish.*

DESCRIPTION: Dark green to gray above, with silvery sides and white belly. Body is heavy and jaw underslung. The 7 or 8 longitudinal stripes are vivid and usually unbroken.

SIZE: Average in most areas is 5-20 pounds, but 30 pounders are fairly frequent catches and Stripers can still exceed 50 pounds on occasion. In the past, fish from 75 to more than 100 pounds were recorded. World record 78 pounds, 8 ounces.

FOOD VALUE: Outstanding; light, rich flesh.

GAME QUALITIES: A very strong and tenacious fighter.

TACKLE AND BAITS: All categories of casting tackle—spinning, baitcasting and fly—are used with effect on small to medium stripers. Bigger fish, however, are most often caught in areas where light tackle is out of place due to current, lure size, casting requirements and other factors. Stout surf outfits—either conventional or spinning—get the call along Atlantic beaches and rocky shores, most of which feature heavy wave action. Light to medium ocean outfits are the best choices for fishing from boats in the deep rips and currents that Stripers favor, and there, wire or leadcore lines may be needed. Spoons, squids, feathers and large surface or swimming plugs all have their uses in Striper fishing, with smaller plugs, jigs and streamer or popping flies getting the nod in calm and reasonably shallow water. A huge array of productive natural baits include various small fish both live and dead, plus eels and marine worms. Dead baits and cutbaits will take Stripers, particularly at night, but live baits are always to be preferred.

FISHING SYSTEMS: Casting; Trolling; Drifting; Still Fishing.

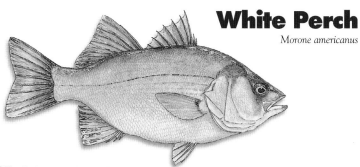

White Perch
Morone americanus

DESCRIPTION: Only vaguely similar in appearance to the much larger Striped Bass, the White Perch sheds its stripes by adulthood and is also flatter. It has two dorsal fins, notched but connected. Coloration is whitish with a greenish tint. Dorsal area is darker.

SIZE: From less than a pound to 2 pounds; rarely to 4 pounds. World record 4 pounds, 12 ounces.

FOOD VALUE: An excellent panfish.

GAME QUALITIES: Spirited for their size.

TACKLE AND BAITS: Ultralight spinning is sportiest. Fly tackle also is productive in many areas, especially late in the day. Often caught with insects or minnows.

FISHING SYSTEMS: Casting; Drifting; Still Fishing.

RANGE: *From North Carolina to Nova Scotia. Very plentiful in New England states.*

HABITAT: *Widespread in bays, estuaries, streams and even in fresh water, but not very numerous, as a rule, along the outside coast. They prefer areas of soft bottom. Plentiful around many bay shorelines and easily caught by youngsters.*

Wreckfish
Polyprion americanus

DESCRIPTION: Deep, flattened body gives it something of the appearance of a giant perch.

SIZE: To at least 100 pounds; maximum not known. World record 156 pounds, 8 ounces.

FOOD VALUE: Excellent.

GAME QUALITIES: Largely untested.

TACKLE AND BAITS: The species is a predator and, at the surface, has been known to take both live and dead fish, plus cutbaits, along with spoons and plugs.

FISHING METHODS: Still Fishing; Casting (Surface).

RANGE: *New England to North Florida. The only commercial fishing ground is located far offshore of the South Carolina coast.*

HABITAT: *Adults are generally found in depths beyond the limits of sporting tackle—around sharp drops along the edge of the Continental shelf. Juveniles are pelagic and occasionally are encountered at the surface.*

Nearly as wide-ranging as the Striped Bass, various members of the Croaker family are familiar to anglers from New England to Florida. Patriarch of the clan is the Red Drum or Redfish, which in many areas exceeds 50 pounds, but at any weight down to only a few pounds is rated as a favorite prize. The Black Drum can grow even bigger than the Red, but does not enjoy quite the same prestige. Spotted Seatrout and Weakfish have hordes of followers and well-deserved reputations as gamefish, while various smaller Croaker species, such as Kingfish (Whitings) and Spot, are usually on hand to provide lots of sport and fine fish dinners to anglers nearly everywhere on the coast.

The Croakers

Red Drum

Black Drum

Spotted Seatrout

Weakfish

Sand Seatrout

Silver Seatrout

Atlantic Croaker

Spot

Northern Kingfish

Southern Kingfish

Gulf Kingfish

Silver Perch

Red Drum

Sciaenops ocellatus

OTHER NAMES:

Redfish
Red Bass
Channel Bass
Puppy Drum

RANGE: *Long Island through the Florida Keys; straggles north to New England.*

HABITAT: *The giants are mostly inhabitants of deeper water, either in bays or offshore, and are seasonally common in the surf over most of their range. Smaller fish may be found nearly anywhere inshore, but they prefer rock or shell areas, or grassy shallows well populated with crustaceans. Large schools of big fish are frequently encountered offshore. Smaller Reds roam into coastal rivers and creeks at any time of year, and in winter may swarm into them, seeking warmer water.*

DESCRIPTION: Adults usually are more bronze than red in overall hue. Smaller specimens may have a pinkish, white appearance. Nearly all show one or more spots at the tail. Scales are large and thick. Big Reds can be confused with large Black Drum; however, the Black Drum has chin barbels.

SIZE: Smaller fish run from a couple of pounds up to 15 pounds or so, but over most of their range they are not too rare at 30 pounds and may at times top 50. World record 94 pounds, 2 ounces.

FOOD VALUE: Up to around 10 pounds, Red Drum are rated among the favorite fish of most anglers. Dark portions of the flesh do not have a strong taste when fresh, but should be trimmed away before cold-storing or freezing. Large Redfish are not very good eating.

GAME QUALITIES: A superior battler, using strength, stamina and fairly long, bullish runs as its main weapons with only rare jumps.

TACKLE AND BAITS: Surf rods and light-to-medium saltwater outfits get the call for beach, bridge, pier and offshore fishing. All kinds of casting tackle, including fly, are successfully used on Reds of all sizes, but mostly, of course, for the smaller fish—say under 20 pounds. Redfish are ravenous feeders that will take live baitfish, crabs and shrimp, and also dead or cut baits. Chunks of Mullet or Menhaden (Bunker) are popular surf baits. Live shrimp, minnows and small crabs (or cut crab) make the very best baits for shallow coastal fishing.

FISHING SYSTEMS: Still Fishing; Drifting; Casting.

Black Drum

Pogonias cromis

DESCRIPTION: Juvenile Drum have black vertical stripes on dusky white sides. Adults are deep bronze to dingy black. All sizes have barbels under the lower jaw. Small Drum can be confused with Sheepshead, which are similarly striped, but the Sheepshead has prominent teeth, which the Drum does not.

SIZE: Average size is among the largest of any coastal sport fish, with specimens weighing 30 to 50 pounds being common along the Mid-Atlantic and South Atlantic coasts, and catches exceeding 75 pounds not awfully rare. Striped juveniles generally weigh 1-10 pounds. World record 113 pounds, 1 ounce.

FOOD VALUE: Drum to about 6 or 8 pounds are as tasty as Red Drum, but bigger ones drop rapidly in quality. The flesh becomes dark, coarse and unappetizing.

GAME QUALITIES: The fight is strong and bullish, but not usually suspenseful or spectacular.

TACKLE AND BAITS: For big Drum, surf tackle and saltwater boat rods are often needed as much for making the necessary presentations as for fighting the fish, which can be caught rather easily on light lines by experienced anglers with a little patience. Any sort of crustacean makes good bait — small whole crabs, halves or quarters of larger crabs, live or dead shrimp. Cut fish and squid may also work well. In most areas, Drum are not good prospects for artificial lures, but can be taken on slowly worked jigs in deep water, or by careful and repetitious presentation of jigs or streamer flies in sight-fishing situations.

FISHING SYSTEMS: Still Fishing; Casting.

OTHER NAMES:

Drum
Striped Drum

RANGE: *New York to the Florida Keys, straggling to Maine.*

HABITAT: *Surf and estuarine areas. Juveniles like shorelines, bar edges and shallows, while bigger fish mostly prefer surf, channels and open water and are pets of bridge and pier fishermen in many areas.*

Spotted Seatrout

Cynoscion nebulosus

OTHER NAMES:

Trout
Speckled Trout
Speck
Spotted Weakfish

RANGE: *New Jersey to the Florida Keys, straggling to Long Island Sound.*

HABITAT: *In warm weather, Spotted Seatrout are most commonly found over grassy or shell-strewn flats, but they inhabit a great variety of water from the surf to coastal rivers and, at times, even roam fairly far offshore. They seek deeper water when the weather gets chilly.*

DESCRIPTION: Many black spots and a large mouth with prominent canine teeth easily identify this popular species. Background color is usually silvery, but can range from dark gray to golden, depending mostly on environment.

SIZE: Typical size is a pound or two, but fish up to 4 pounds are common in nearly all areas of its range, and specimens exceeding 10 pounds may pop up in some places. The maximum potential is more than 15 pounds, with most of the giants coming from Florida's East-Central Coast. World record 17 pounds, 7 ounces.

FOOD VALUE: Very good.

GAME QUALITIES: Although not particularly strong or swift, Seatrout are hard strikers and tussle well on light tackle. Only the big ones are drag-takers, but all put up a showy, surface-thrashing fight, and occasionally jump clear of the water.

TACKLE AND BAITS: Light gear is a must for best sport, with spinning and baitcasting tackle capable of covering all situations. Fly tackle is also effective, especially, of course, when fishing the shallows. Nearly all popular natural baits work well — strips of cut fish or squid, plus live and dead shrimp or small live fish. Productive lures include soft plastic baits, plastic-tail jigs, topwater plugs and underwater plugs retrieved in jerk-and-pause fashion. For fly fishermen, large streamers of almost any sort produce strikes, especially if flashy material is tied in. Poppers sometimes get great action in shallow water.

FISHING SYSTEMS: Drifting; Still Fishing; Casting.

Weakfish

Cynoscion regalis

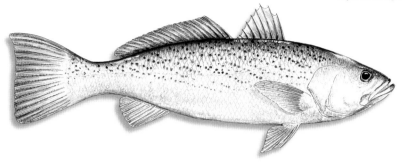

DESCRIPTION: Very similar in appearance to the Spotted Seatrout, except that the spots are very tiny and arranged in diagonal lines. The same prominent canine teeth are present. Overall color is gray or bluish above, silvery below. As with the Seatrout, coloration can vary according to surroundings.

SIZE: The average is 2 or 3 pounds, with 6-pounders fairly common. The potential ranges from more than 10 to the longtime record, but such big fish are now scarce, although their numbers are slowly increasing once more. World record 19 pounds, 2 ounces.

FOOD VALUE: Very good.

GAME QUALITIES: Less of a surface brawler than the Speckled Trout, but very strong and capable of making several long runs during a fight on light tackle.

TACKLE AND BAITS: Spinning, baitcasting, light saltwater tackle and, often, surf gear. Fly fishing usually difficult, but can sometimes be productive. Weakfish bite a variety of invertebrate baits, including shrimp, marine worms, crabs and squid, as well as live small fish and strips of fish. Leading lures include spoons, tin squids, jigs, and swimming plugs. Jig-and-bait combinations work very well in deep fishing.

FISHING SYSTEMS: Still Fishing; Drifting; Casting; Trolling.

OTHER NAMES:
Squeteague
Gray Trout
Tiderunner
Northern Trout

RANGE: *From about Cape Canaveral in Central Florida to New England. Prime grounds extend from Cape Hatteras to Long Island Sound.*

HABITAT: *Prefers deep water and is most often fished in channels and deeper ports of bays but roams to shallow flats at times, following food supply. Also encountered in the surf and in coastal streams, particularly marshy creeks.*

Sand Seatrout

Cynoscion arenarius

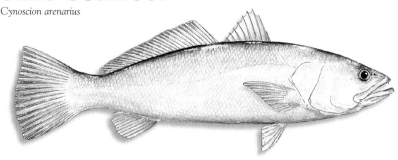

OTHER NAMES:

**White Trout
Sand Trout
Silver Trout**

RANGE: *Florida.*

HABITAT: *Most are caught in deep water with sand or shell bottom. Sometimes taken on shallow flats, along with Spotted Seatrout.*

DESCRIPTION: Although it can be confused with the Weakfish, this fish is smaller and not widely distributed. It also lacks spots or other markings. Color is tan or yellowish above and silver below. Canine teeth present.

SIZE: Usually one-half to 1 pound; rarely exceeds 2. World record 6 pounds, 2 ounces.

FOOD VALUE: Smaller ones make tasty panfish. Those over a pound or so produce mild-flavored fillets.

GAME QUALITIES: Fairly strong for its size, but sporty only on the lightest tackle.

TACKLE AND BAITS: Spinning tackle is best. Productive baits include shrimp, live or dead, and small strips of fish or squid. Small leadhead jigs are tops as artificials.

FISHING SYSTEMS: Still Fishing; Drifting; Casting.

Silver Seatrout

Cynoscion nothus

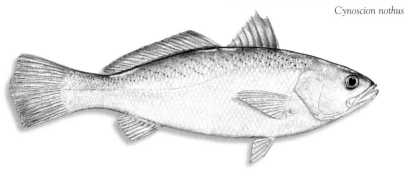

DESCRIPTION: So similar in appearance to the Sand Seatrout that it takes a count of the fin rays to positively distinguish them, but the angling fraternity doesn't much care. The Silver is even smaller and the back is steely blue rather than brownish.

SIZE: Averages 6 to 10 inches; seldom tops 1 pound.

FOOD VALUE: Fine panfish.

GAME QUALITIES: Small size limits its ability to resist.

TACKLE AND BAITS: Any kind of tackle, but the lighter the better. Use small hooks and pieces of shrimp, squid or cut fish. Small leadhead jigs produce at times.

FISHING SYSTEMS: Still Fishing; Drifting; Casting.

OTHER NAMES:
Sand Trout
White Trout

RANGE: *From Florida to Virginia, but not too prominent anywhere.*

HABITAT: *Basically, this is a fish of open water. Many are caught by anglers during late winter and spring, when they invade the deep channels of harbors and bays.*

Atlantic Croaker

Micropogonias undulatus

OTHER NAMES:

**Croaker
Hardhead**

RANGE: *From South Florida to Massachusetts.*

HABITAT: *Likes sand or shell bottom; a common surf fish. Popular pier catch in most areas.*

DESCRIPTION: Overall silver or gold background with sometimes indistinct wavy lines on upper sides. Small barbels on underside of lower jaw. Similar in shape to the Red Drum.

SIZE: In the southern part of its range it averages a pound or less, with a top weight of perhaps 3 pounds. From Cape Hatteras northward, and particularly in Virginia and Maryland, 3-pounders are fairly common and 5-pounders possible. World record 3 pounds, 12 ounces.

FOOD VALUE: Excellent. Small ones make good panfish. Fillets of larger specimens are fine-grained and mild flavored.

GAME QUALITIES: Strong for their size but unspectacular.

TACKLE AND BAITS: Many are caught on surf tackle, but light spinning or baitcasting gear will provide more sport when conditions permit. Croakers prefer any kind of dead bait—shrimp, squid, cut fish, pieces of crab or mollusk.

FISHING SYSTEMS: Still Fishing.

Spot
Leiostomus xanthurus

DESCRIPTION: The forked tail and prominent spot behind the gill cover makes this fellow easy to identify. The color is brassy, with wavy lines on the upper surfaces. Underside is white.

SIZE: The spot seldom reaches a pound. Average length is 6 or 8 inches.

FOOD VALUE: Very good. One of the most popular panfish for the table.

GAME QUALITIES: Spunky but too small to resist vigorously.

TACKLE AND BAITS: Anything goes here, from a child's pole or handline to all sorts of rods and reels. Obviously, light tackle and small hooks will do the best job in fishing for Spot. It is just as hard to go wrong in choosing bait. Marine worms, cut fish, shrimp and squid are popular choices, but meat scraps from the table work about as well.

FISHING SYSTEMS: Still Fishing.

OTHER NAMES:
Spotted Croaker
Norfolk Spot
Mizzouki Croaker

RANGE: From South Florida to southern New England. Most abundant from Georgia to New Jersey.

HABITAT: Very common in the surf, and also widely distributed in bays and estuaries. Reliable fun on a great many piers and bridges.

Northern Kingfish

Menticirrhus saxatilis

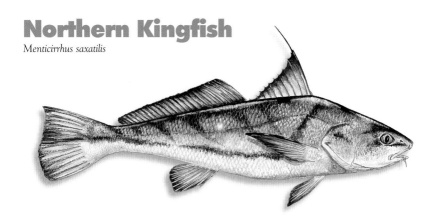

OTHER NAMES:

Whiting
Northern Whiting
Sea Mullet

RANGE: *From South Florida to New England, but most common north of Cape Hatteras.*

HABITAT: *Sandy bottom of surf, channels, passes and bayshores.*

DESCRIPTION: A long spine on the dorsal fin distinguishes this fish from the other two Kingfishes (Whitings) which follow. Overall color is also the darkest of the three—dusky or nearly black, with blacker bars on the upper sides. Chin barbel present.

SIZE: Usually under a pound, but may top 2 pounds. World record I pound, 10 ounces.

FOOD VALUE: Good.

GAME QUALITIES: Very strong for its size.

TACKLE AND BAITS: Light surf tackle is the best choice, but all kinds of gear can be used in various settings. Best baits include small crabs and marine worms, plus cut shrimp, squid and fish. Seldom fished with artificial lures but will readily take small jigs.

FISHING SYSTEMS: Still Fishing.

Southern Kingfish

Menticirrhus americanus

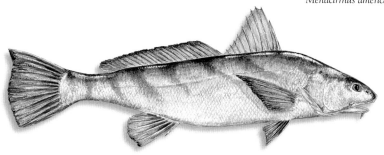

DESCRIPTION: The head is large in proportion and with a chin barbel. The belly is flat. Much lighter in color, overall, than the Northern Kingfish, it is yellowish on top with silvery sides and indistinct blotches.

SIZE: Usually less than a pound; sometimes 2 pounds. World record 2 pounds, 5 ounces.

FOOD VALUE: Bland but good.

GAME QUALITIES: Runs well against very light tackle.

TACKLE AND BAITS: Best baits are small crabs, such as sand fleas, and pieces of shrimp or squid. They will hit small jigs and flies. On bright, calm days, they can be sight-fished along the edge of the surf. Spinning, baitcasting and even fly tackle are productive in calm situations, but many beaches call for heavier surf gear.

FISHING SYSTEMS: Still Fishing; Casting.

OTHER NAMES:

Whiting
Southern Whiting

RANGE: *From New England to South Florida. Most abundant from Central Florida to New Jersey.*

HABITAT: *Roams sandy bottom. Abundant surf fish.*

Gulf Kingfish

Menticirrhus littoralis

OTHER NAMES:

Silver Whiting
Gulf Whiting

RANGE: *As the name suggests, this is the dominant Whiting of the Gulf Coast, but is also a fixture of Atlantic waters, being plentiful from Florida to Cape Hatteras and extending to Chesapeake Bay.*

HABITAT: *Likes hard sand bottom of surf, channels, and inlets.*

DESCRIPTION: Unlike the two species named earlier, the Gulf Kingfish has no blotches or other markings on the sides, but is an overall silvery gray color. The tail is tipped in black.

SIZE: Averages slightly larger than the other two species, often weighing a pound and sometimes running to 3 pounds. World record 3 pounds.

FOOD VALUE: Good.

GAME QUALITIES: Very strong fighter on light line.

TACKLE AND BAITS: Good baits include shrimp, squid, sand fleas and crabs. They will hit small jigs and flies and can be sight-fished along the edge of the surf when waves are low and visibility good. Spinning, baitcasting and even fly tackle are productive under calm conditions, but heavier surf gear may be needed on many beaches.

FISHING SYSTEMS: Still Fishing; Casting.

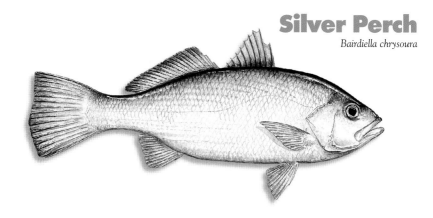

Silver Perch
Bairdiella chrysoura

DESCRIPTION: Overall appearance is silver with a grayish or steely back. The fins are yellowish. The Silver Perch is often called a "Trout" but lacks the prominent canine teeth of the Seatrouts. It is also easy to confuse with the White Perch (Chapter 1).

SIZE: Seldom exceeds 6 or 8 inches.

FOOD VALUE: An excellent panfish.

GAME QUALITIES: An avid striker but too small to provide much sport.

TACKLE AND BAITS: The very lightest tackle with small hooks and pieces of shrimp, fish or squid. They readily hit small jigs or other tiny artificial lures.

FISHING SYSTEMS: Still Fishing; Casting.

OTHER NAMES:
Yellowtail
Sugar Trout
Silver Trout

RANGE: New England to Central Florida; most common from North Florida to Cape Hatteras.

HABITAT: Prefers protected water of bays, estuaries and coastal streams. Abundant in coastal rivers and streams during the winter.

The fish in this chapter may be wildly different in size, distribution and habitat, but they have two things in common: (1) they are all superb gamesters in a particular size class, and (2) they are either the only member of their families found along the Atlantic Coast, or else the only one of any interest to anglers. Exceptions are the Tarpon and Ladyfish, which do share a family tie. Out of this sterling group, the Bluefish stands out as the popularity king. It is as far-ranging as the Striped Bass and, in many cases, is caught from the same water on the same baits — especially in the surf and around rocks or rips. By contrast, the Bonefish is the most restricted geographically, yet it draws the attention of anglers from all over the world. Dolphin, of course, are roamers of the deep sea, while most of these other rugged individuals commonly swim within easy range of small-boat or shore anglers.

Rugged
Individuals

Great Barracuda

Bluefish

Bonefish

Cobia

Dolphin

Ladyfish

Tarpon

Tripletail

Great Barracuda

Sphyraena barracuda

OTHER NAMES:

Cuda

Sea Pike

RANGE: *Cape Hatteras to South Florida; strays farther north.*

HABITAT: *The Barracuda is at home almost anywhere in warmer waters, from shorelines and bays out to the deep blue. From Central Florida northward, the Great Barracuda is seldom encountered except offshore, usually over wrecks or reefs. A similar species, the Northern Barracuda or Sennet, occurs close to shore as far north as New England, but is a much smaller fish of little interest to anglers. It grows to perhaps 18 inches and has no bold markings on its side.*

DESCRIPTION: The pointed head with a jaw full of jagged teeth is an easy identifier of the Barracuda. The silvery sides are marked by black blotches. The body is elongated.

SIZE: Juveniles up to a few pounds frequent the flats and shores of southern Florida and Bermuda. In deeper waters, most Barracuda run from 10 to 20 pounds. Individuals up to 40 pounds are not unusual, and the maximum size exceeds 80 pounds. World record 84 pounds, 14 ounces.

FOOD VALUE: Excellent to 5 pounds or so. Large fish have been known to carry Ciguatera poison.

GAME QUALITIES: The Great Barracuda ranks among the most spectacular of fighters, frequently mixing fast and fairly long runs with greyhounding jumps. It can also fight deep with good strength and stamina.

TACKLE AND BAITS: In shallow waters of Florida or Bermuda, spinning and baitcasting tackle are ideal, and fly tackle will also take plenty of Cuda. For offshore trolling or wreck fishing, ocean tackle up to the 30-pound class provides good sport with larger Cuda. Casting tackle can also be used with effect over a wreck or artificial reef when the fish are at the surface. Tube lures work best for the caster, but surface plugs, flyrod poppers, shiny spoons, leadhead jigs and streamer flies incorporating shiny mylar strips often succeed. Live fish make the very best natural baits, with the more active varieties of baitfish being preferable.

FISHING SYSTEMS: Trolling; Casting; Still Fishing.

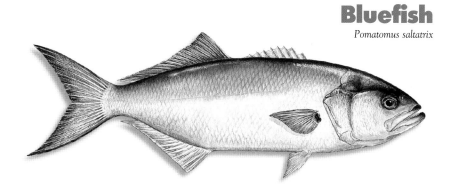

Bluefish
Pomatomus saltatrix

DESCRIPTION: Color is steel blue shading to silvery white below. Dark spot usually shows at base of pectoral fin. Large mouth with prominent teeth. Forked tail.

SIZE: Common at any weight from less than a pound to 10 or 12 pounds. Not rare to 20 pounds, especially along the Middle and North Atlantic Coast. Maximum weight can exceed 30 pounds. World record 31 pounds, 12 ounces.

FOOD VALUE: Fair to very good. Small Bluefish make fine table fare broiled or pan-fried, if iced promptly and eaten soon—the same day they are caught, if possible. Larger fish should be bled and iced. After filleting, the dark meat should be trimmed away.

GAME QUALITIES: Pound-for-pound, Blues are outstanding gamesters. They jump nimbly, if not too frequently, also making long runs.

TACKLE AND BAITS: Stout ocean tackle with lines up to 30 or 40-pound test is not too heavy for the bigger fish offshore. Light casting and spinning tackle is adequate in most instances for Blues of average size around shorelines and in protected waters. Surf or surf-spinning gear must be used, of course, on the beach, and are also good choices for many ocean piers. Heavy leaders are usually necessary to prevent clipoffs by the Blue's sharp teeth. Stout monofilament leaders usually suffice, but wire can be used too. Bluefish are ravenous, and will take virtually any popular bait—live and cut fish, cut squid, live shrimp. As for artificial lures, fast retrieves work best.

FISHING SYSTEMS: Casting; Trolling; Still Fishing.

OTHER NAMES:
Blue
Chopper
Tailor

RANGE: *Seasonally common from Nova Scotia all the way to South Florida.*

HABITAT: *Small Bluefish—to around 5 or 6 pounds—frequent bays, estuaries and outside shorelines. Larger fish prefer deeper water farther offshore, often congregating in rips, but they do not hesitate to follow the bait inshore and many big fish are caught by surf fishermen, from Cape Hatteras to Maine.*

Bonefish
Albula vulpes

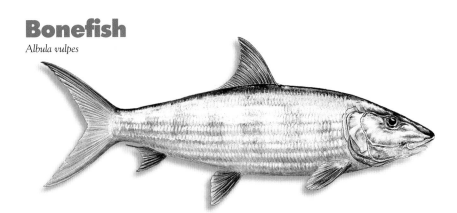

OTHER NAMES:

Boneyfish
White Fox
Gray Ghost

RANGE: *A tropical species, it is largely confined to South Florida and Bermuda, although wandering specimens have been encountered as far north as New England.*

HABITAT: *Although they stick to deep water most of the time, Bonefish regularly explore the shallows for food—and that is where most fishing for them takes place. Over mud, sand or grass flats, or near calm beaches, feeding Bonefish can be sighted and cast to. They may also gather in large schools over fairly deep, soft bottom, where their feeding stirs up patches of silt or "mud."*

DESCRIPTION: The back is dark green. The sides are silver with prominent scales; the head pointed and the tail forked. The body is thick and muscular.

SIZE: Averages 3 or 4 pounds, but is fairly common to 10 pounds and can exceed 15 pounds. World record 19 pounds.

FOOD VALUE: Bonefish are seldom eaten. They are indeed very bony, to say nothing of being too highly prized as gamefish to kill for a mediocre dinner.

GAME QUALITIES: The long-distance running capability of a Bonefish in a foot or so of water is legendary. In deep water, the battle is rough and bullish.

TACKLE AND BAITS: Classic sight-fishing for Bonefish makes use of either spinning outfits, preferably with light, 7-8-foot rods and lines up to 10-pound test. Light baitcasting outfits can also be effective in practiced hands. Bonefish rank among the top favorites of fly fishermen, whose standard gear is an 8-weight outfit. Lighter fly rods get some spot use, if wind conditions allow, and 9-weight outfits are not too heavy for good sport. Live shrimp, small crabs, and cut pieces of shrimp, crab or other shellfish make the best natural baits. Most productive spinning lures are horizontally flattened jigs, often called skimmer jigs, weighing up to ¼ ounce. These plane upward on the retrieve and keep the hook upright. Most fly rodders prefer very small flies with monofilament weedguards on No. 2 or even No. 4 hooks, but simple bucktails or streamers on No. 1 or 1/0 hooks have taken many Bonefish.

FISHING SYSTEMS: Casting; Still Fishing.

Rachycentron canadum

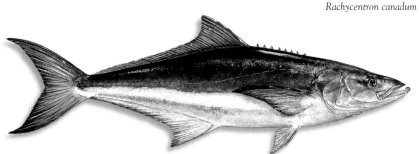

DESCRIPTION: Cobia are dark and torpedo shaped and, in the water, look so much like sharks that even experienced anglers are sometimes briefly fooled. The skin is also leathery and shark-like, but the flattened head, frontal jaws and absence of teeth are the obvious differences. A dark stripe from the gills to the tail is more vivid in small specimens.

SIZE: Common from 20 to 50 pounds; sometimes up to 80 and possibly 100 or more. World record 135 pounds, 9 ounces.

FOOD VALUE: Excellent, but with a unique taste that is unlike most fish. Great for baking or smoking.

GAME QUALITIES: Cobia are rugged fighters but individualistic, and so the tussle can be rather unpredictable. Usually, a big fish will get off several long and fairly fast runs, and resist doggedly for long periods in between them.

TACKLE AND BAITS: Since Cobia are notorious for wrapping lines around buoys and wreck structure, most anglers use saltwater gear, with 30-pound-test line or heavier, when live-baiting in such spots. Surf tackle is the best bet for pier fishing—and for boat fishing when long casts with heavy lures are called for. When gaffed "green" (untired), Cobia can—and often do—smash up the inside of a boat. Jigs, ranging from ½ ounce to 2 ounces in weight, depending on casting distance or depth needed, and large streamer flies are the most-used artificials. Baitfish, such as Pinfish, Menhaden, Mullet, Cigar Minnows, Grunts and Jacks are nearly always chosen by live-baiters.

FISHING SYSTEMS: Still Fishing; Casting; Trolling; Drifting.

OTHER NAMES:
Ling
Cobbeo
Lemonfish

RANGE: New England to South Florida.

HABITAT: Cobia can be found, at times, anywhere from shallow flats of bays and coastal waters, out to the open sea. They winter in subtropical waters and migrate northward in the spring. Dramatic annual runs occur as far north as Virginia, but in every part of the coast, Cobia are likely to be found hanging around navigation markers, wrecks and artificial reefs, where they swim both at the surface and down deep. They also escort wandering Mantas and other large rays. Juveniles are frequently caught over inshore flats, and Cobia of all sizes are common catches on ocean piers.

Dolphin

Coryphaena hippurus

OTHER NAMES:

Dorado
Dolphinfish
Mahi Mahi

RANGE: *Florida to Massachusetts, perhaps straggling farther north in late summer. Dolphin are warmwater fish, progressively more plentiful to the south.*

HABITAT: *The open sea. Many are caught by blind-trolling, but anglers much prefer to seek out weedlines, rafted weeds or floating objects of any sort — the larger the better. Dolphin frequently hang around such flotsam, which provides cover for baitfish. Feeding birds may also point the way to Dolphin schools.*

DESCRIPTION: Dolphin are among the most colorful of gamefish, usually a bright mix of deep green or blue with bright yellow. The colors are changeable when the fish are feeding or otherwise excited, and dark vertical stripes may also be present. Small dark spots pepper the sides. In males, the head is blunt. Females show a more rounded silhouette, as do both sexes of the only other species of Dolphin — the small **Pompano Dolphin**, *Coryphaena equisetis*.

SIZE: Schooling Dolphin tend to be the same size, which may range from a pound or so to perhaps 20 pounds. Most large Dolphin run singly or in male-female pairs. Males (bulls) are always larger, often attaining 50 pounds in weight and sometimes exceeding 80 pounds. World record 88 pounds.

FOOD VALUE: Excellent. The white flesh is mild but flavorful, and suitable for any method of cooking.

GAME QUALITIES: Here, too, the Dolphin ranks among the very best. It combines long, strong runs with spectacular jumps and dogged stubbornness.

TACKLE AND BAITS: Spinning, baitcasting and fly tackle are popular for school Dolphin, but fish from 20 pounds upward are no patsies on ocean trolling tackle up to the 30-pound class. Private-boat anglers typically seek to find Dolphin either by trolling and staying alert for visual signs, or simply by running fast and covering as much water as possible while searching for such signs. Once a school is located, it can usually be kept around the boat by restrained chumming with cutbait and/or by keeping at least one hooked fish in the water. Big or wise fish may insist on live baits.

FISHING SYSTEMS: Trolling; Drifting; Casting.

Ladyfish

Elops saurus

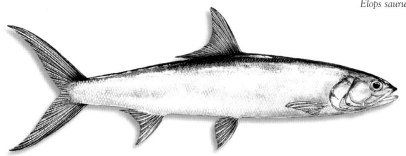

DESCRIPTION: The Ladyfish is silvery overall, with a greenish back and a single, prominent dorsal fin, deeply forked tail and large, scoop-shaped lower jaw

SIZE: Most run a pound or so. A 4-pound Ladyfish is a whopper, although they have been reported to 7 pounds or more. Where the archaic name "Ten-Pounder" comes from is a mystery. World record 6 pounds.

FOOD VALUE: Poor. The flesh is mushy and there are numerous small bones.

GAME QUALITIES: Among the best for their size, Ladyfish get off the wildest jumps of any small fish and are also strong runners that can zip surprising amounts of line from the spools of light spinning or casting tackle.

TACKLE AND BAITS: Frequently found schooling at the surface or in very shallow water, Ladyfish make excellent targets for the fly fisherman. They will hit small poppers and many different streamer flies, but the best are Glass Minnow imitations with monofilament-wrapped hook shanks. They are great sport, too, on light and ultralight spinning tackle. Most are caught on cut strips, small live fish or live shrimp by anglers fishing for something else, particularly Seatrout, but Ladyfish are ready strikers on most artificial lures of appropriate size. Jigs and small topwater plugs rate high.

FISHING SYSTEMS: Casting; Drifting; Still Fishing.

OTHER NAMES:

Skipjack
Chiro
Ten-Pounder

RANGE: Most common in Florida. Occurs, though not plentifully, north through the Carolinas.

HABITAT: Ladyfish may be encountered anywhere from the ocean beaches to inlets, bays and coastal streams, where they sometimes wander into completely fresh water. Although often plentiful on shallow grassflats, they are found in channels and deep holes as well, seeming to have no preferred surroundings so long as food is present. They are avid night feeders around lighted areas of piers and docks. Wherever Ladyfish are found, they usually are in schools, ranging from a few fish to, at times, hundreds.

Tarpon

Megalops atlanticus

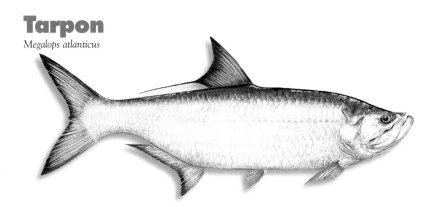

OTHER NAMES:

Silver King
Sabalo

RANGE: *Florida to Long Island; straggles to New England. Fishable numbers gather seasonally in every Atlantic state from Virginia southward, and also in Bermuda.*

HABITAT: *In most of the Atlantic states, Tarpon are seen only from early summer through fall. The same is true for much of Florida, although the southern end of that state has year-around fishing for them. Major fishing efforts for big Tarpon are directed at live-baiting in large passes, inlets, channels and river mouths. Sight-fishing with fly and casting tackle is practiced in several areas of Florida, mostly on shallow flats but sometimes in inlets and channels. From Central Florida northward, the bulk of the Tarpon fishing is done off the Atlantic beaches and around piers, although some fish do enter deeper inside bays and river mouths. Tiny juveniles inhabit landlocked canals, ponds and ditches, but are seldom caught north of Florida.*

DESCRIPTION: Adults are massive fish with large scales. Bright silver is the dominant color, although the back is green and the forked tail dark. The mouth is large and scoop-jawed, and a lone streamer runs off the last ray of the dorsal fin.

SIZE: From a foot to about 75 pounds, on average, although big fish of 100 pounds are numerous, and a 200-pounder is always a possibility. World record 283 pounds, 4 ounces.

FOOD VALUE: None.

GAME QUALITIES: Tarpon are world-famous for the spectacle and frequency of their jumps. Giant Tarpon don't quite match the acrobatics of the smaller ones, but when hooked in shallow water, they leap almost as much and with even more fury.

TACKLE AND BAITS: Tarpon come in all sizes; therefore, all sizes and descriptions of tackle find good use. Anglers seeking big fish in passes, channels, deep bays, piers and surf choose surf rods or stout boat tackle, with saltwater reels and lines testing at least 30 pounds, and preferably 50. All sizes of spinning, baitcasting and fly tackle get lots of play in areas where small and medium-size fish are encountered. The same types of gear, although of heavier proportions, are also used to cast for big fish on shallow flats in Florida. Typical fly tackle consists of a 10-12-weight outfit with 16-pound leader and a heavy tippet of 80- or 100-pound monofilament. Anglers using heavy tackle prefer live baits, such as Mullet, Menhaden, Pinfish, Spot, or even crabs.

FISHING SYSTEMS: Casting; Trolling; Drifting; Still Fishing.

Tripletail
Lobotes surinamensis

DESCRIPTION: The Tripletail's name derives from the similarity and near juxtaposition of the dorsal, caudal and anal fins, resembling three tails. The deep and rounded shape gives it the appearance of an enormous Bluegill or similar panfish. Color varies but is usually mottled shades of brown. The head is concave. The mouth is apparently small but is capable of opening wide to engulf fairly large prey.

SIZE: The average is from 2 to about 12 pounds, and few exceed 30 pounds. World record 42 pounds, 5 ounces.

FOOD VALUE: Excellent.

GAME QUALITIES: Despite its strange silhouette, the Tripletail is a fine gamefish. When hooked, it often surprises the angler by jumping — looking something like a platter sailing through the air. It will strike either artificial lures or live baits. Its runs are generally short but zippy, and, like Cobia, it often makes an effort to foul the line around any pilings or floats.

TACKLE AND BAITS: Spinning, baitcasting gear provides the best and most spectacular sport with Tripletails, but saltwater outfits with lines up to 30-pound test are not out of place for big fish in tight places. Fly fishermen have a good chance, too, with spotted fish. Streamer flies, plastic and bucktail jigs and mirror plugs are among the pet lures. Best natural baits are live shrimp and small live fish. Strip baits and dead shrimp are also acceptable for hungry Tripletail.

FISHING SYSTEMS: Still Fishing; Drifting; Casting

OTHER NAMES:

Drift Fish
Leaf Fish

RANGE: May be found at sea as far north as Massachusetts, but the inshore sport fishery is restricted mostly to Florida.

HABITAT: The Tripletail drifts with ocean currents and might be spotted by offshore anglers anywhere along the Atlantic Coast, usually around weedlines or alongside floating debris, lying on their sides and resembling floating leaves. In Florida, and occasionally in other South Atlantic waters, they can also be found close to shore or even in large bays, usually hanging around navigation markers or trap floats.

Human beings are either right-handed or left-handed but, having no hands, Flounders are either right-eyed or left-eyed when viewed from the "eyed" side with the dorsal fin on top. Despite their flattened shape and bottom-hugging habits, most Flounders are aggressive predators and fine gamefish that will chase down and strike artificial lures as well as live or dead natural baits. King of the family is the potentially huge Halibut, but smaller varieties, headed by the Winter Flounder and the Summer Flounder (Fluke), provide far more sport for far more fishermen up and down the Atlantic Coast.

The Flounders

Atlantic Halibut

American Plaice

Winter Flounder

Yellowtail Flounder

Summer Flounder

Southern Flounder

Gulf Flounder

Atlantic Halibut

Hippoglossus hippoglossus

RANGE: *Subpolar Canada to New York, straggling a bit farther south on occasion. Most are taken near Newfoundland, both from the famed Grand Banks and other waters nearer the coast.*

HABITAT: *Rocky bottom in from 200 to more than 1000 feet deep.*

DESCRIPTION: Right-eyed. Upper side is dark, ranging from green or brown to almost black in the largest specimens. The lateral line is straight for most of its length but curves high over the pectoral fin. The huge mouth is well equipped with curved teeth. The tail is concave.

SIZE: The Halibut is one of the two largest bottom fish of the Atlantic Coast—the other being the Jewfish of southern waters. Although reported to more than 500 pounds in the past, the largest Halibut of recent times have been in the 200-300-pound range. Average weight is from 50 to 150 pounds. World record 355 pounds, 6 ounces.

FOOD VAUE: Excellent.

GAME QUALITIES: Relatively few sport fishermen will ever get to tangle with a big Halibut, but those who do will have their hands full. They are very difficult to bring up from the bottom and, even at the surface, remain full of fight and must be handled carefully.

TACKLE AND BAITS: It is nearly impossible for sportsmen to target Halibut. The few taken usually fall to anglers seeking Cod far offshore of New York, New England and the Canadian Maritimes. The heaviest of bottom-fishing gear is obviously called for, with lines of at least 40-pound test. Halibut are mostly fish-feeders but have taken the full range of baits used on partyboats, including clams, squid and other shellfish.

FISHING SYSTEMS: Drifting; Still Fishing.

American Plaice

Hippoglossoides platessoides

DESCRIPTION: Right-eyed. A close relative of the Halibut, but easily distinguished by much smaller size and by the tail fin, which is rounded rather than concave. Color is rusty or brown. The mouth is very large.

SIZE: Up to about 3 feet and 12 or 15 pounds.

FOOD VALUE: Excellent.

GAME QUALITIES: Plaice are strong fighters but often overpowered by heavy tackle.

TACKLE AND BAITS: Difficult to target, most Plaice are caught incidentally while bottom-fishing aboard party-boats. Any sort of mollusk, such as clams and sea-worms, makes good bait, as do crabs.

FISHING SYSTEMS: Drifting; Still Fishing.

OTHER NAMES:
American Dab
Sand Dab

RANGE: *Extends from Labrador to Cape Cod; not as widely distributed as the Halibut.*

HABITAT: *Mostly deep water, but found close to shore at times. Like other Flounders, it prefers soft or sandy bottom.*

Winter Flounder

Pseudopleuronectes americanus

OTHER NAMES:
Flattie
Black Flounder
Blackback
  Flounder
Lemon Sole
Mud Dab

RANGE: *One of the most common and most popular sport fish from Nova Scotia to Chesapeake Bay, it also occurs, less plentifully, all the way north to Labrador and south to Georgia.*

HABITAT: *Widely distributed, from shorelines and coastal streams out to 100 feet of water or more. Always prefers soft bottom—mud, sandy mud or even gravel. Scattered patches of grass add appeal.*

DESCRIPTION: Right-eyed. Color varies a great deal, from blotchy brown or greenish-blue to black—depending on bottom type. The mouth is very small and the tail is round. The lateral line is nearly straight.

SIZE: Usually 1 to 2 pounds. Up to 5 or 6 pounds on occasion, especially offshore. World record 7 pounds.

FOOD VALUE: Excellent.

GAME QUALITIES: Not much of a challenge, but fun on light tackle.

TACKLE AND BAITS: Light spinning tackle provides the most sport, especially when fishing from the many shoreline spots where Winter Flounder can be taken—docks, piers, banks and seawalls. Somewhat heavier tackle, such as baitcasting, medium spinning or light saltwater gear, may be needed when fishing near shore in strong currents, because heavy sinkers may be required. For Winter Flounder, the bait must be kept right at bottom. The fish don't range widely when feeding, so the best angling approaches are either drifting or else anchoring and chumming with crushed shellfish, such as clams, crabs or oysters. The same shellfish make good baits, but the most popular of all are marine worms—bloodworms and sandworms. Very small hooks—No. 6 is a common choice—are needed because this Flounder cannot open very wide.

FISHING SYSTEMS: Still Fishing; Drifting.

Yellowtail Flounder

Limanda ferrugineus

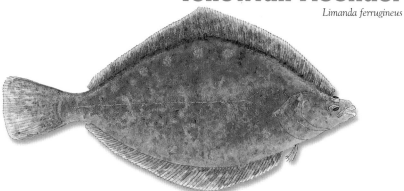

DESCRIPTION: Right-eyed. Brown in color, with orange or red spots that turn rusty after death. The dorsal, caudal and anal fins are edged in yellow. The mouth is small.

SIZE: 2 pounds is about tops.

FOOD VALUE: Excellent.

GAME QUALITIES: A sluggish fighter, it is nearly always caught on too-heavy gear to provide much sport.

TACKLE AND BAITS: Like the other deepwater Flounders, the Yellowtail shows up on a sportsman's line only occasionally, as the result of grab-bag fishing. Crustaceans, mollusks and worms are all acceptable baits.

FISHING SYSTEMS: Drifting; Still Fishing.

OTHER NAMES:
Rusty Dab

RANGE: Gulf of St. Lawrence to Chesapeake Bay. Most plentiful off Nova Scotia and New England.

HABITAT: Usually found at 100 feet or deeper, over mud or hard sand bottom.

Summer Flounder

Paralichthys dentatus

OTHER NAMES:

Fluke
Northern Fluke
Flattie
Doormat

RANGE: *From Maine to North Florida, where it is rare. Peak abundance occurs from Cape Cod to Georgia.*

HABITAT: *Nestles into soft bottom but likes to have grassbeds or other cover close by. Often numerous around bridges and piers. In the more northerly portions of its range, many are caught fairly far offshore, in water 30 feet deep or more.*

DESCRIPTION: Left-eyed. Color is generally olive or brown, but can vary widely according to color of the bottom on which the fish hides. Eye-like spots called ocelli are liberally sprinkled on most specimens, and there are always five or more such spots, contrasted to the Gulf Flounder, which has only three.

SIZE: Averages 2-4 pounds, although specimens to 10 or 12 pounds are not rare. Potential maximum probably exceeds 25 pounds. World record 22 pounds, 7 ounces.

FOOD VALUE: Excellent.

GAME QUALITIES: Strong and very active for a Flounder. Often chases artificial lures vigorously before striking.

TACKLE AND BAITS: The large, toothy mouth indicates that fish are a prominent part of its diet; therefore, Finger Mullet and other small baitfish make the best baits, although shrimp, crabs and worms are also good. Jigs and swimming plugs, retrieved slowly, are the most productive artificials. Spinning, baitcasting and light saltwater outfits are all appropriate, depending on personal choice and, perhaps, the casting distance required.

FISHING SYSTEMS: Still Fishing; Drift Fishing; Casting.

Southern Flounder
Paralichthys lethostigma

DESCRIPTION: Left-eyed. Prominent eye-like spots (ocelli) seen on the Fluke and the Gulf Flounder are missing.

SIZE: Virtually matches the size of the Fluke, averaging 2-4 pounds. World record 20 pounds, 9 ounces.

FOOD VALUE: Excellent.

GAME QUALITIES: Hard striker and strong fighter.

BAITS AND TACKLE: Under most conditions, light spinning or baitcasting tackle is more than adequate, but for "Doormats" around jetties and inlets, stouter rods and lines should be used, especially for livebaiting.

FISHING SYSTEMS: Still Fishing; Casting; Drifting.

OTHER NAMES:
Southern Fluke
Flattie
Doormat

RANGE: *North Carolina to South Florida. Shares much of its range with the Fluke.*

HABITAT: *Generally encountered in relatively shallow areas, but is taken from channels as well. It likes soft bottom near such cover as bars or rubble. Many are caught around bridges.*

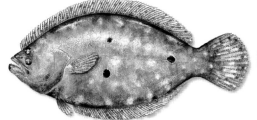

Gulf Flounder
Paralichthys albigutta

DESCRIPTION: Left-eyed. This fish is quite similar in coloration to the Southern Flounder, but it is easily distinguished by its three ringed spots (ocelli).

SIZE: Smaller than both of the preceding species, the Gulf Flounder averages 1 or 2 pounds. World record 6 pounds, 4 ounces.

FOOD VALUE: Excellent.

GAME QUALITIES: Commendable, but not so strong as their bigger relatives.

TACKLE AND BAITS: Try light or ultralight spinning and baitcasting tackle. Somewhat heavier casting gear, and light boat rods, can be used in deeper water around wrecks. They spend most of their time snuggled in soft sand, but all the left-eye Flounders are voracious predators.

FISHING SYSTEMS: Still Fishing; Casting; Drifting.

OTHER NAMES:
Flattie

RANGE: *Despite its name, the Gulf Flounder is found on the Atlantic Coast from North Carolina to South Florida, as well as in the Gulf of Mexico.*

HABITAT: *Like its close relatives already discussed, the Gulf Flounder can be found on open sandy flats, but generally prefers to stick near cover, such as grassbeds and the edges of rocks and rubble; also docks, bridges and piers, wherever the bottom is suitably soft.*

ne of the most storied of tropical and subtropical gamefish, the Snook is largely a Florida species, although a rare specimen or two may wander farther north on occasion. We're speaking of the Common Snook. Actually, three smaller species are also found in Florida, but are little known, even to most Floridians. Superficially, they all look alike because of the silvery color and black lateral line. None of the lesser types has been reported north of the Sunshine state.

The Snooks

Common Snook

Fat Snook

Swordspine Snook

Tarpon Snook

Common Snook

Centropomus undecimalis

OTHER NAMES:

Lineside
Robalo
Ravillia

RANGE: *Found in dependable numbers only in the lower half of Florida, although sometimes caught as far north as Jacksonville, or even the Georgia coast.*

HABITAT: *Mainly encountered along the Atlantic Coast of South Florida around inlets, ocean piers, surf, bridge and dock pilings and the shorelines of rivers and canals.*

DESCRIPTION: A tapered snout, underslung lower jaw, large fins and a jet-black stripe on the lateral line makes any Snook easy to pick out of a fishy lineup. But the differences between this large species and the three smaller ones to follow are a bit more subtle. The adult Common Snook can be identified by size alone, although confusion arises when comparing juveniles against adults of the other kinds. Color of the dorsal surface is usually dark, often black. Sides are silvery in sea-run fish. The fins are yellow.

SIZE: Average is about 3 to 15 pounds. Snook weighing 20 to 30 pounds are common, especially during summer spawning season. Usual maximum is about 40 pounds, but the potential is to 60 or more. World record 53 pounds, 10 ounces.

FOOD VALUE: Excellent. The meat is white, mild.

GAME QUALITIES: All-around fighting ability is first-rate, with big specimens delivering long and repeated runs, often ending in boiling half-jumps. Smaller fish leap higher and more frequently. A major tactic of all sizes is to foul the line on any handy object.

TACKLE AND BAITS: Baitcasting outfits, medium-heavy spinning gear, and light saltwater outfits are best suited to live-baiting in the inlets and around pilings. Fly fishermen choose large streamers and poppers, while hard-lure casters rely heavily on jigs, spoons, swimming plugs and topwater plugs. Live Mullet and Pinfish head the list of natural baits.

FISHING SYSTEMS: Still Fishing; Casting; Trolling; Drift Fishing.

Fat Snook
Centropomus parallelus

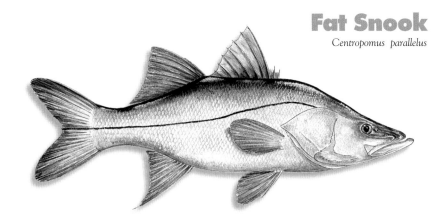

DESCRIPTION: As the name denotes, this one is proportionately deeper-bodied than the Common. Coloration, however, is about the same.

SIZE: Sometimes reaches 24 inches in length, but most run 12-16 inches. World record 9 pounds, 5 ounces.

FOOD VALUE: Seldom caught in legal size, but excellent.

GAME QUALITIES: A spirited jumper and tough for its size.

TACKLE AND BAITS: Although usually a catch of opportunity, the best gear, given a choice, would be the lightest spinning, baitcasting and fly tackle, with small jigs, surface and swimming plugs; also streamer flies and popping bugs. Natural baits are live shrimp or small live fish.

FISHING SYSTEMS: Still Fishing; Casting; Trolling.

OTHER NAMES:
**Cuban Snook
Calba**

RANGE: South Florida. Not common anywhere, but most likely to hit a bait around Miami or Fort Lauderdale, or in the Florida Keys.

HABITAT: Small canals, streams and backwaters.

Swordspine Snook

Centropomus ensiferus

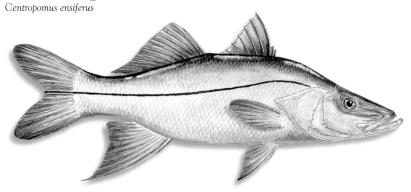

OTHER NAMES:
Little Snook

RANGE: *South Florida. The rarest Snook species, it is occasionally taken in protected waterways.*

HABITAT: *Most have been caught from freshwater ponds and canals of the Miami area and the Upper Keys.*

DESCRIPTION: All species of Snook have long, hard spines on the front of the anal fin, but that of the Swordspine is easily the longest-extending, when folded against the body, past the beginning of the caudal fin. In other species, this spine does not reach the caudal.

SIZE: Seldom longer that a foot. World record 1 pound, 5 ounces.

FOOD VALUE: Not relevant.

GAME QUALITIES: Spunky but tiny.

TACKLE AND BAITS: The lightest spinning, baitcasting and fly tackle with small jigs and flies; live shrimp.

FISHING SYSTEMS: Still Fishing; Casting.

Tarpon Snook

Centropomus pectinatus

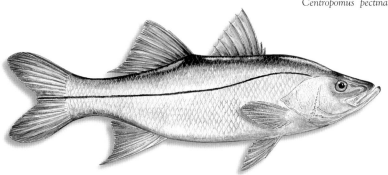

DESCRIPTION: The body is flattened. The name comes from the similarity of the head to that of a small Tarpon.

SIZE: Usually a foot or so. Can reach at least 20 inches. World record 3 pounds, 2 ounces.

FOOD VALUE: Insignificant.

GAME QUALITIES: A good battler for its size.

TACKLE AND BAITS: The lightest spinning, baitcasting and fly tackle, with small jigs, surface and swimming plugs, or streamer flies. Live shrimp is the best natural bait.

FISHING SYSTEMS: Still Fishing; Casting; Trolling.

RANGE: *South Florida and the Keys.*

HABITAT: *Like the Common Snook, it likes to lurk near bridge and dock pilings of calm inland waterways; also around mangroves and other shoreline cover.*

When is a Jack not a Jack? When it's a delicious Pompano or a prestigious Permit. The point is that various members of this huge and popular family wear names other than Jack, which often adds to their desirability in the angler's mind, but not necessarily to their sporting qualifications. Pound for pound, nearly every member of this group is an outstanding battler, and some of them carry a great many pounds indeed. However, a few very small Jacks, known as Scads, aren't big enough to rank as sport fish, but still serve the angling world very well as bait. Those are included in Chapter 22.

The Jacks

African Pompano

Almaco Jack

Banded Rudderfish

Bar Jack

Blue Runner

Crevalle Jack

Florida Pompano

Greater Amberjack

Horse-eye Jack

Leatherjack

Lesser Amberjack

Lookdown

Palometa

Permit

Pilotfish

Rainbow Runner

Yellow Jack

African Pompano

Alectis ciliaris

OTHER NAMES:
Threadfish
Threadfin
Cuban Jack

RANGE: Florida to Nova Scotia, but not easily fishable except in the South.

HABITAT: The best fishing is found around deep wrecks and sharp offshore dropoffs, but they are also taken on shallow reefs. Young Threadfins may be found drifting far offshore.

DESCRIPTION: The adult is a large, vertically flattened fish with bright pearlescent sides. The head is distinctively blunt. In juveniles the forward rays of the dorsal and anal fins are very long and threadlike, and these "streamers" sometimes hang on into early adulthood, although they usually are lost as the fish grows. Young "Threadfish" of a couple pounds and less were once thought to be a different species.

SIZE: Adults are common at 15-30 pounds and grow to at least 50 pounds. World record 50 pounds, 8 ounces.

FOOD VALUE: Excellent.

GAME QUALITIES: The African fights much like other big Jacks, but uses its flat side to even greater advantage, and exhibits a peculiar, circling tactic that puts the angler to a rough test. All in all, it is one of the toughest light-tackle battlers.

TACKLE AND BAITS: Most African Pompano are caught by jigging deep in the vicinity of wrecks or offshore dropoffs with spinning and baitcasting tackle; or by fishing deep with light ocean tackle and live bait. They generally hang too deep to interest fly fishermen, although a few have been caught by blind-fishing over wrecks with sinking lines, or by chumming them to the surface with live chum. A variety of heavy jigs and large streamers will work, especially if trimmed with silvery Mylar. Pinfish, pilchards and similar small fish are the live baits of choice. Africans are occasionally caught by trolling over the reefs with feathers or rigged baits.

FISHING SYSTEMS: Drifting; Trolling; Still Fishing.

Almaco Jack

Seriola rivoliana

DESCRIPTION: Could be confused at a glance with the Greater Amberjack, due to similar coloration and the band through the eye, but the body of the Almaco is deeper and more compressed. Also, the dorsal and anal fins are sickle-shaped and proportionately longer.

SIZE: Common from 10 to about 30 pounds; may reach 75 or more. World record (Atlantic) 78 pounds.

FOOD VALUE: Excellent.

GAME QUALITIES: As tough as the Greater Amberjack.

TACKLE AND BAITS: Spinning, baitcasting and light ocean tackle with lines up to 20-pound test are ideal; however, since most Almacos are caught in Amberjack habitat, heavier gear often is used. Small live baits are seldom refused. Jigs work too.

FISHING SYSTEMS: Drifting; Still Fishing.

OTHER NAMES:
**Almaco
Horse-eye
 Amberjack**

RANGE: *Florida to Cape Cod, but not prominent north of Cape Hatteras. Also Bermuda.*

HABITAT: *Largely the same as the Greater Amberjack.*

Banded Rudderfish

Seriola zonata

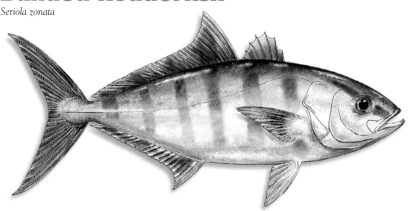

OTHER NAMES:

Slender Amberjack

RANGE: *Florida to Cape Cod.*

HABITAT: *Unlike the Pilotfish, which prefers offshore waters, the Banded Rudderfish is more coastal. It is often found around navigation aids near shore, and in deep channels and bays.*

DESCRIPTION: As evidenced by the dark line through the eye, the banded Rudderfish is a small member of the Amberjack clan. This helps distinguish it from the similarly marked Pilotfish. Also, the Rudderfish is banded only on the sides of its body, not on the fins.

SIZE: Usually a foot or less; may grow to 2 feet.

FOOD VALUE: Good.

GAME QUALITIES: Like all Amberjacks, a tough fighter.

TACKLE AND BAITS: Very light spinning, baitcasting or fly outfits, with small jigs, spoons or streamer flies. Will take any live baitfish of suitable size, and also shrimp and small strips.

FISHING SYSTEMS: Drifting; Still Fishing.

Bar Jack

Caranx ruber

DESCRIPTION: A blue or black stripe extending from behind the head into the lower lobe of the tail identifies this Jack, which has the streamlined shape of the Yellow Jack, but is mostly silver in color. Hard scutes forward of tail.

SIZE: Most run about 1 pound. Maximum is around 5 or 6 pounds.

FOOD VALUE: Excellent if red portions of meat are trimmed.

GAME QUALITIES: About the same as the Blue Runner, which means very tough for its size.

TACKLE AND BAITS: Most sport will be obtained with light spinning tackle and small jigs. Also a good fly fish that will take most Bonefish flies. Best natural baits are live shrimp and live small fish, but cut strips of fish or squid will also work at times.

FISHING SYSTEMS: Casting; Trolling; Drifting; Still Fishing.

OTHER NAMES:

Reef Runner
Bahamas Runner

RANGE: Common in South Florida and Bermuda; may roam north to Long Island.

HABITAT: Likes sandy beach areas, clear, grassy flats and coral reefs.

Blue Runner

Caranx crysos

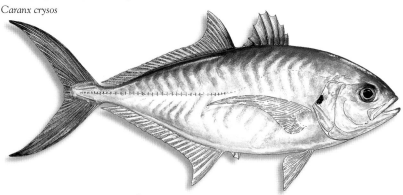

OTHER NAMES:

Runner
Hardtail Jack
Blue Jack

RANGE: *Florida to Nova Scotia. Common from Cape Cod southward.*

HABITAT: *Nearly everywhere, from coastal creeks and bays to the deep sea.*

DESCRIPTION: Similar in shape to the Crevalle, but with a more gently rounded head. The color ranges from steel blue to light green with white underparts. The shape is somewhat more streamlined than the Crevalle's and the head not as blunt. The hard tail scutes are present, however.

SIZE: Blue Runners often roam in big schools, made up of fish averaging from one-half to 1 pound in weight. Occasionally, they can hit 4 pounds or more—usually offshore. World record 11 pounds, 2 ounces.

FOOD VALUE: Somewhat better than the Crevalle, but seldom eaten.

GAME QUALITIES: Like all Jacks, Blue Runners are superb fighters for their size. Many an angler has struggled to land a rather small Blue Runner, thinking all the while that he is fighting something at least two or three times as large.

TACKLE AND BAITS: Most sport will be obtained with light spinning using live shrimp, cut pieces of fish or small artificial jigs. They also accept streamer flies and poppers.

FISHING SYSTEMS: Trolling; Drifting; Casting; Still Fishing.

Crevalle Jack

Caranx hippos

DESCRIPTION: Deep, compressed body. The head is blunt, with a black spot on the rear edge of the gill cover. This, along with the hard scutes, deep body and sickle tail make the Crevalle easy to identify. The color is dirty yellow with whitish undersides.

SIZE: Jacks may run from hand size to more than 50 pounds. World record 57 pounds, 14 ounces.

FOOD VALUE: Poor. The meat is dark red.

GAME QUALITIES: None better for strength and stamina. The battle is unspectacular but dogged, the usual pattern being a fairly long first run, followed by shorter, circling runs and stubborn resistance. Jacks use their flat sides to good advantage.

TACKLE AND BAITS: Since most of the fish encountered are rather small, they can be taken on the full range of light tackle. If larger Jacks—say 10 pounds or more—enter the picture then stout spinning, bait-casting and fly rods should be used, with lines no less than 8-pound test. If you go after the really big Jacks of 20 pounds and upward, you won't be undergunned with the heaviest of spinning, casting and fly tackle, or light and medium saltwater outfits. Small Jacks greedily accept most small natural baits, live or dead, along with jigs, streamer flies, surface plugs and popping bugs; the big fellows, however, are smarter and more picky. They prefer fast-moving prey, so to get strikes you may have to resort to fresh and frisky live fish, or retrieve your artificial lures rapidly, noisily or both.

FISHING SYSTEMS: Casting; Trolling; Drifting.

OTHER NAMES:
Jack
Hardtail
Jack Crevalle

RANGE: Most common from Cape Hatteras southward, but roams as far north as Cape Cod.

HABITAT: Jacks may appear at any time and in any area from the deep reefs to bays and rivers. They run in schools, and the smaller the fish, the larger the school. The biggest Jacks often cruise in pairs and are usually found in or near major inlets and around offshore wrecks and reefs, but huge fish also storm into bays, rivers and canals where they chase Mullet and often herd the prey against seawalls. In Florida, most of the giant Jacks are caught in the Palm Beach and Key West areas.

Florida Pompano

Trachinotus carolinus

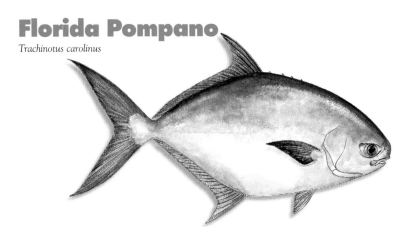

OTHER NAMES:

Carolina Pompano

RANGE: *Occurs north to Cape Cod at times but is common only in the Carolinas, Georgia and Florida.*

HABITAT: *Most Pompano are caught from the surf or from ocean piers, but they also come into bays, where they patrol the deeper water and small channels around sandbars and grassflats.*

DESCRIPTION: The overall coloration is silver with yellow on the throat and underside. The dorsal fin is dark; the other fins yellow. No hard scutes. Pompano can easily be confused with small Permit, but their bodies are not so deep and they lack the Permit's black blotch under the pectoral fin.

SIZE: Averages 1 pound, with 2-pounders not uncommon. Can run as high as 8 pounds or so. World record 8 pounds, 1 ounce.

FOOD VALUE: Ranks among the best. The flesh is firm, white and rich.

GAME QUALITIES: Also top-rank. The fight surpasses that of a Jack, being at least equally rugged, but with longer and faster runs.

TACKLE AND BAITS: For surf and pier fishing, the lightest surf spinning tackle is ideal. Many beaches are calm enough so that ordinary casting tackle—spinning, baitcasting, and even fly—will suffice. By far the best natural bait is a live sand flea (sand crab), but Pompano also will bite live shrimp or fiddler crabs and—with varying dependability—dead sand fleas, dead shrimp, clams and cut squid. They are ready strikers of small artificial jigs, the favorite being quarter-ounce or half-ounce models with short nylon skirts. Fly fishermen catch Pompano with weighted flies, tied with epoxy heads or lead eyes.

FISHING SYSTEMS: Still Fishing; Casting; Drifting.

Greater Amberjack

Seriola dumerili

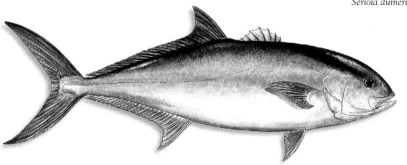

DESCRIPTION: A dark oblique line through the eye, ending at the first ray of the dorsal fin, is a family birthmark of the Amberjack clan. Another is the absence of hard scutes on the caudal peduncle. The Greater Amberjack is brownish or gold in color, with a thick, heavy body.

SIZE: Around many wrecks, schools of fish weighing less than 10 pounds are common. More typically, however, Amberjack run from 20 to 60 pounds, with fish as heavy as 100 pounds not too rare. Maximum is 150 or more. World record 155 pounds, 12 ounces.

FOOD VALUE: Excellent, smoked or fresh.

GAME QUALITIES: Amberjack are usually hooked in deep water, and they instantly power-dive even deeper if they can. They are very strong and defy lifting. Fairly long runs can also occur early in the fight. Their stamina matches their strength.

TACKLE AND BAITS: Most are caught aboard charterboats and partyboats by patrons using heavy rods and reels with lines testing 50 pounds or more—and are no patsies, even then. Experienced light-tackle anglers can successfully battle them with spinning and baitcasting rigs, and even fly rods, but good lines and rods with plenty of backbone are necessities. Around wrecks, they frequently follow hooked fish to boatside, and sometimes rise to the top voluntarily. Then they can be cast to with surface plugs, spoons, jigs or big flyrod streamers and poppers. Live chum will also draw Amberjack from the depths.

FISHING SYSTEMS: Drifting; Trolling; Casting.

OTHER NAMES:

Amberfish
AJ

RANGE: *Mostly from Florida to Cape Hatteras, but ranges as far north as Cape Cod. Also Bermuda.*

HABITAT: *Adults are common at various depths, from reefs several hundred feet deep to fairly shallow wrecks and reefs. Big ones also come close to shore at times, particularly in South Florida and Bermuda. Artificial reefs and wrecks often harbor large schools.*

Horse-eye Jack

Caranx latus

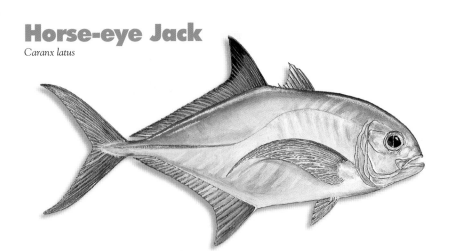

OTHER NAMES:

Big-eye Jack

RANGE: *Florida to Chesapeake Bay.*

HABITAT: *More of an open-water species than the Crevalle, it is found over the reefs and near the beaches; also in channels, bays and harbors where the water is not too turbid.*

DESCRIPTION: Looks much like the Crevalle in silhouette but the head is not so blunt. The color is also different, being silvery on the sides and dark gray to black above. The fins are also blackish as opposed to the yellow tinge of the Crevalle. Hard scutes forward of tail. As the name indicates, the eyes are very large.

SIZE: Commonly up to 6 pounds and may reach nearly 20 pounds. World record 29 pounds, 8 ounces.

FOOD VALUE: About as poor as the Crevalle.

GAME QUALITIES: Great power and stubbornness, and especially strong in water deep enough so that its flat sides can be used to advantage.

TACKLE AND BAITS: Good targets for all light tackle—spinning, baitcasting and fly. Surface plugs often provide spectacular hits. Jigs and spoons produce well. Live baitfish are fine, of course, but the Horse-eye usually isn't too particular to take dead baits or strip baits.

FISHING SYSTEMS: Casting; Trolling; Drifting; Still Fishing.

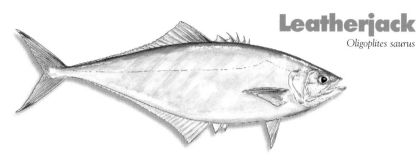

Leatherjack
Oligoplites saurus

DESCRIPTION: Not the most obvious characteristic, but the one an angler should be most aware of, are sharp spines on the dorsal and anal fins that can administer very painful puncture wounds. The shape is slender and compressed, with pointed head and large jaws for its size.

SIZE: A few inches, rarely as much as a foot.

FOOD VALUE: None.

GAME QUALITIES: Poor.

TACKLE AND BAITS: Unfortunately, the Leatherjack will take many different small baits and lures offered for Mackerel and other desirable species.

FISHING SYSTEMS: Not fished for deliberately.

OTHER NAMES:

**Skipjack
Leatherjacket**

RANGE: *Florida to Maine; not common north of Cape Hatteras.*

HABITAT: *Open waters near shore, and also in bays and up rivers. Often found in company with schools of Mackerel, Bluefish or Jack, feeding on the same small fry as the larger fish.*

Lesser Amberjack
Seriola fasciata

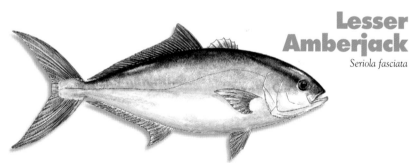

DESCRIPTION: This little fellow is virtually a copy of the Great Amberjack, except for size. The most obvious difference is that the band through the eye of the Lesser Amberjack stops noticeably forward of the dorsal fin.

SIZE: Probably never gets larger than a foot long.

FOOD VALUE: Minimal.

GAME QUALITIES: At least as good as other Jacks, ounce for ounce.

TACKLE AND BAITS: Ultralight spinning and fly tackle. Small jigs, plugs and flies.

FISHING SYSTEMS: Drifting; Still Fishing.

RANGE: *Florida to Cape Cod.*

HABITAT: *Offshore waters, usually around weedlines and flotsam. May occur closer to shore as well; however, the huge majority of very small Amberjack caught on shallow reefs and wrecks are simply juveniles of the Greater Amberjack.*

Lookdown

Selene vomer

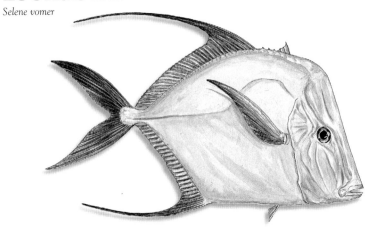

OTHER NAMES:

Horse-head

RANGE: *Florida to Nova Scotia.*

HABITAT: *Nearly anywhere in shallow coastal waters, but most common around bridge and dock pilings, navigation markers, and in channels and canals, where they frequently gather under shoreside lights at night.*

DESCRIPTION: This and a similar species, the **Moonfish**, *Selene setapinnis*, are blunt-headed silvery fish of similar size, appearance and habits. Moreover, they are often found in company with each other, which adds to the angler's confusion. The Lookdown is the more common of the two and has a sloping, concave head and long streamers running off the dorsal and anal fins. These streamers, however, are not nearly so long and flowing as those of the juvenile African Pompano. The head of the Moonfish is less blunted than that of the Lookdown, and all its fins are short.

SIZE: Usually less than a pound, but they often reach 2 pounds and can run to 3 or 4 on rare occasion. World record 4 pounds, 10 ounces.

FOOD VALUE: Both species are tasty panfish.

GAME QUALITIES: Aggressive strikers and good fighters for their size, they are prone to running in circles like their big cousin, the African Pompano.

TACKLE AND BAITS: Ultralight or very light spinning and fly tackle allow the most fun. Both fish are good strikers on small jigs and tiny plugs. They also take live minnows and shrimp, but don't much care for dead baits.

FISHING SYSTEMS: Casting; Still Fishing.

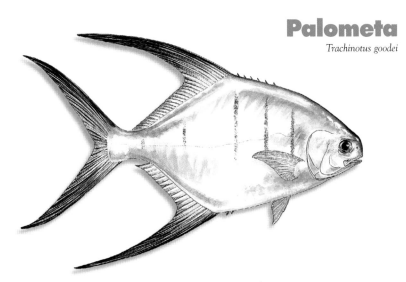

Palometa

Trachinotus goodei

DESCRIPTION: Vertical dark bars and long rays of the dorsal and anal fin make this Pompano easy to distinguish. The dark bars are sometimes visible over lighter sand when the fish itself cannot be seen.

SIZE: Probably doesn't grow much past 2 pounds. Most weigh a pound or less. World record 1 pound, 3 ounces.

FOOD VALUE: Excellent.

GAME QUALITIES: Small but spunky and fast; also wary and hard to fool.

TACKLE AND BAITS: Performs best on very light spinning and fly tackle. Jigs and flies must be small—No. 1 at the most—for consistent success. Small crabs, sand fleas and shrimp are top baits.

FISHING SYSTEMS: Still Fishing; Casting.

OTHER NAMES:
Longfin Pompano
Pompanito
Gafftopsail Pompano

RANGE: *Fishable mostly in Florida and Bermuda, but wanders to New England.*

HABITAT: *Likes clear water with sandy bottom near sheltered beaches and sandbars. No longer plentiful anywhere along the Atlantic Coast, not even Florida.*

Permit

Trachinotus falcatus

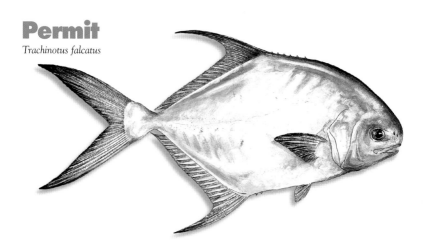

OTHER NAMES:

Round Pompano
Great Pompano

RANGE: *The great majority of Permit are caught in Florida, but numerous catches have been recorded from Cape Hatteras southward, and a few north to Cape Cod.*

HABITAT: *Some Permit are found in the surf and around inlets. Many inhabit reef areas and wrecks. Sight fishing in the shallows is pretty much confined to South Florida and the Keys.*

DESCRIPTION: The body is deeper and rounder in shape than that of the Pompano. The tail is very large and sickle-shaped. Scutes absent. Silver overall, with black blotch on side under the pectoral fin.

SIZE: Fish weighing 20 or 30 pounds are common, both on inshore flats and offshore wrecks and reefs. World record 56 pounds, 2 ounces.

FOOD VALUE: Small fish are excellent. Large ones are edible but should be released.

GAME QUALITIES: Considered by many as perhaps the best shallow-water gamefish in the world, combining long distance runs with great power.

TACKLE AND BAITS: In deep water, a large Permit can give an excellent account of itself against saltwater tackle and lines up to 30-pound test, but are sportiest on rather stout spinning and baitcasting outfits. The glamorous approach is to stalk them by sight— Bonefish style—on shallow flats, and cast directly to them. Rather light spinning, baitcasting and fly tackle can be used in the shallows—provided the angler has a good supply of line or is able to chase the fish. Best natural bait is any sort of small live crab. Dead pieces of crab and lobster also work well. Live shrimp are often accepted. Skimmer-type Bonefish jigs are the best spinning lures. Once a Permit takes up the chase, the lure should be stopped and allowed to sink to the bottom. Weighted flies—some of them resembling skimmer jigs made of epoxy—are fished in similar manner.

FISHING SYSTEMS: Casting; Still Fishing.

DESCRIPTION: A more slender shape and banded fins, including the tail fin, help distinguish the Pilotfish from the similar Banded Rudderfish, which is one of the Amberjacks.

SIZE: Usually a foot or so; grows to 2 feet.

FOOD VALUE: Good but usually too small for most anglers to bother with.

GAME QUALITIES: On suitably light tackle, a tough fighter.

TACKLE AND BAITS: Readily takes small jigs and streamer flies. Only very light outfits provide much sport.

FISHING SYSTEMS: Offshore drifting.

RANGE: *Entire coast and Bermuda.*

HABITAT: *Offshore waters. The name refers to its habit of accompanying sharks and other large animals—seemingly as pilots, but actually as opportunistic feeders.*

Rainbow Runner

Elagatis bipinnulata

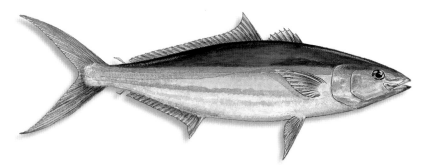

OTHER NAMES:

Rainbow Jack
Spanish Jack

RANGE: *Not too common anywhere along the Atlantic Coast, it likes warm water and is most likely to be encountered off the South Atlantic states and Bermuda.*

HABITAT: *The deep ocean.*

DESCRIPTION: This is the most brightly colored of all Jacks. It has blue and yellow full-length stripes against a blue background, with white underparts. The shape is slender and the head pointed. No hard scutes.

SIZE: Varies from a couple of pounds to 15 or 20 pounds, with individuals of roughly the same size forming large schools. World record 37 pounds, 9 ounces.

FOOD VALUE: Excellent.

GAME QUALITIES: Despite difference in shape, the Rainbow Runner is as tough for its size as any Jack, besides which, it makes faster runs and may even jump.

TACKLE AND BAITS: Most of the rare catches are made by blind trolling with heavy tackle, but if you ever get the chance to fish selectively for Rainbow Runners, you can use spinning, baitcasting and light ocean rigs. Small live fish and small rigged baits, such as ballyhoo and strips are the best bets. They are difficult to take by casting, but can be coaxed to a jig, spoon or swimming plug.

FISHING SYSTEMS: Trolling; Casting.

Yellow Jack

Caranx bartholomaei

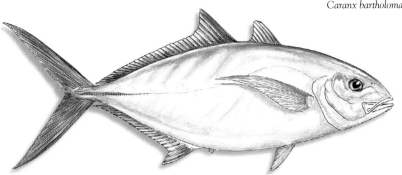

DESCRIPTION: This streamlined Jack is quite colorful, with bluish back, bright yellow markings on the sides, and yellow fins. Hard scutes are present on the caudal peduncle.

SIZE: The usual range is 1 to 5 pounds, but occasional specimens can push 20 pounds. World record 23 pounds, 8 ounces.

FOOD VALUE: Excellent. Unlike some other Jacks, most of the fillet meat is light in color, with the red portion confined to the center line and easily trimmed away.

GAME QUALITIES: Like other Jacks, a rugged and stubborn fighter, but gets off some fairly long runs when hooked on the flats.

TACKLE AND BAITS: Spinning, baitcasting and light saltwater outfits will give good sport. Small live fish are the best natural baits. Biggest Bar Jack have been caught on topwater plugs over channels and shallow reefs, and on deep jigs in up to about 120 feet of water. On the flats, the bigger Bar Jack are moody but smaller ones eagerly hit live shrimp, bonefish jigs and other small lures.

FISHING SYSTEMS: Casting; Trolling; Drifting; Still Fishing.

OTHER NAMES:
Bar Jack

RANGE: *Primarily Florida to Cape Hatteras; reaches Cape Cod on occasion.*

HABITAT: *Likes clear water. Small fish are commonly found inshore on shallow flats. Big fish stick mostly to deep water around reefs and dropoffs.*

Atlantic Salmon are anadromous—meaning that they spend most of their lives at sea, but go upriver to spawn. With Trout, however, the sea-run life is optional. Although they can happily spend their entire lives in fresh water, certain populations in certain areas are entirely anadromous. Brook and Brown Trout that run to sea are generally called "Sea Trout" or "Salters," whereas sea-run Rainbows are called "Steelhead." Confusingly, however, the situation in our northern waters is not so clear-cut. While there definitely are true sea-run Brookies in the Canadian Maritime Provinces—and possibly a few New England rivers as well—many of the Rainbows, Browns and Brookies caught in river mouths, bays and estuaries from Maine to New York are simply "freshwater" Trout that roam into the salt in search of food. From a sporting standpoint, though, who cares?

Trout and Salmon

Atlantic Salmon

Brown Trout

Brook Trout

Rainbow Trout

Atlantic Salmon

Salmo salar

RANGE: Fishable throughout the Maritime Provinces of Canada, and in a few rivers in Maine. Natural range once extended south to New York.

HABITAT: Most fishing for Salmon takes place in rivers during the spawning runs of spring and summer. They are also taken in estuaries and tidal pools of the rivers prior to beginning their runs.

DESCRIPTION: Appearance varies during several distinct life phases. Adult Salmon fresh from the sea are heavy-bodied and bright silver, with blue or blue-black backs and many small, black spots above the lateral line. The spots are not round but of irregular outline, many of them x-shaped. Young adult fish (grilse) returning from the sea for the first time have forked tails, which become square in later years. Adult salmon returning to sea after spawning (kelts) are dark and thin and often called "Black Salmon."

SIZE: Grilse average 4-8 pounds. Adults run 10-20 pounds, with a rare catch pushing 50 pounds. Atlantic Salmon of 100 pounds have been recorded. World record 79 pounds, 2 ounces.

FOOD VALUE: Ranks among the elite of food fish.

GAME QUALITIES: Unequaled. Combine the strength of a powerful marine fish with the swift waters where most Salmon are hooked and you have some of the world's most challenging light-tackle fishing—especially after you add great stamina and a few spectacular jumps to the mix.

TACKLE AND BAITS: Fly fishing is the only legal method in Maine and the majority of Canadian streams. Despite volumes devoted to the "best" Salmon flies, local preferences always rule. The usual choice in fly gear is a No. 8 or No. 9 outfit, with a rod at least 9 feet long. In the rare instances where spinning tackle is used in Western Atlantic waters, bright spoons and spinners are the most productive. Strangely, Salmon do not feed in the rivers, but strike only by instinct. At sea, they feed voraciously.

FISHING SYSTEMS: Casting.

Brown Trout

Salmo trutta

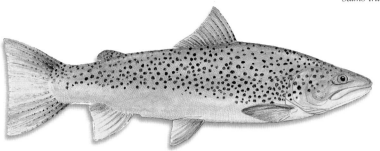

DESCRIPTION: Typical freshwater coloration is tan or light brown with dark brown spots that are often ringed in orange or red. Sea-run fish are silvery and their spots are smaller and less distinct. They could easily be confused with small Salmon (grilse) were it not for the absence of x-shaped spots. Definite identification is provided by two rows of teeth on the roof of the mouth, as opposed to a single row on Salmon.

SIZE: Although recorded to 100 pounds in Europe and to more than 40 in America, few of our sea-run fish reach 10 pounds, and the average size is less than 2 pounds. World record 40 pounds, 4 ounces.

FOOD VALUE: Excellent.

GAME QUALITIES: A strong fighter and considered the most difficult member of its family to entice to a hook.

TACKLE AND BAITS: Fly fishermen do best with small streamer flies, around Size 8 or 10, that imitate silvery baitfish, or with shrimp flies in the same sizes. Small spinners and spoons work well for spin fishermen. Similarly, minnows and shrimp head the list of natural baits.

FISHING SYSTEMS: Casting.

OTHER NAMES:
European Brown Trout
Sea Trout

RANGE: Labrador to New York.

HABITAT: Brown Trout venture regularly, but rather haphazardly, into salt water from numerous rivers in New York, New England, Nova Scotia and Newfoundland. They are fished both in the estuaries and in the rivers.

Brook Trout

Salvelinus fontinalis

OTHER NAMES:

Brookie
Speckled Trout
Salter

RANGE: Labrador to New York, but the major sea-run fisheries are found in Newfoundland and other northern waters of the Canadian Maritimes.
HABITAT: Coastal rivers and estuaries.

DESCRIPTION: Worm-like markings called vermicula on the dorsal surface and dorsal fin make freshwater Brookies easy to spot, but the "Salters," like most sea-run trout, lose most of their markings and become silvery overall, with only a few pinkish spots.

SIZE: Usually less than a pound, but Salters often run 2 pounds and occasionally to 5 pounds or so. World record 14 pounds, 8 ounces.

FOOD VALUE: Excellent.

GAME QUALITIES: Many sea-run Brookies are taken by Salmon fishermen on tackle too heavy for them to show their abilities. On light fly rods, however, they are famous scrappers.

TACKLE AND BAITS: Like Salmon, the Salters are willing to take a variety of flies that do not necessarily imitate local food items. But, unlike Salmon, they also look for food, so small shiny streamers and shrimp flies work well, both in the rivers and the estuaries.

FISHING SYSTEMS: Casting.

Rainbow Trout

Oncorhynchus mykiss

DESCRIPTION: The bright colors and famous lateral red streak of the inland Rainbow fades away in sea-run fish, although a pinkish cast may remain along the lateral line. The upper surface is bluish and there are small spots on the side, mostly above the lateral line.

SIZE: Sea-run fish average a pound or two in weight, with a 5-pounder being a good one. World record 42 pounds, 2 ounces.

FOOD VALUE: Varies with diet but usually very good.

GAME QUALITIES: Excellent fighter and strong jumper.

TACKLE AND BAITS: Light fly rods are best, with rather small flies and streamers in a variety of patterns, many with combinations of red-and-white or green-white or silver-white.

FISHING SYSTEMS: Casting.

OTHER NAMES:
Steelhead

RANGE: *Coastal mostly in the Canadian Maritime Provinces. Although sometimes called "Steelhead," the smaller Atlantic Coast Rainbows are not nearly as migration-minded as their Great Lakes and western relatives of that name.*

HABITAT: *Coastal rivers and estuaries.*

Major identifying characteristics of the Wrasses are protruding teeth and large, heavy scales. Underneath those scales, however, lie delicious fillets—a fact that is well known to devotees of the Hogfish—a large and spectacular-looking Wrasse of southern waters. Strangely, though, many anglers who like to fish for the northern Tautog are unaware of its fine table quality because they consider its appearance so unappetizing that they refuse to try it. Too bad for them! The other Wrasses covered below are the colorful Green Wrasse, or Puddingwife, which is taken fairly often by southern reef anglers, and the Cunner, which is seldom viewed as anything other than a bait-stealing pest.

The Wrasses

Tautog
Cunner
Hogfish
Puddingwife

Tautog

Tautoga onitis

OTHER NAMES:

Blackfish
Rockfish

RANGE: *Nova Scotia to the Carolinas.*

HABITAT: *Inshore around rocks, wrecks, pilings and jetties.*

DESCRIPTION: Adult males have thick, protruding lips and are dark overall, often nearly black. Females have more gently rounded heads and are mottled grey and black in color. Single dorsal fin extends from above the pectoral to the caudal peduncle. No scales on gill cover.

SIZE: Commonly 2 to 5 pounds. Frequently reaches 10 pounds or more and can exceed 20 pounds. World record 25 pounds.

FOOD VALUE: Excellent, although shunned by many because of outward appearance and dark bones.

GAME QUALITIES: A very strong, if not spectacular, fighter.

TACKLE AND BAITS: Light ocean tackle, baitcasting outfits and spinning gear are all useful, but rods should always be stout in order to set the hook in a Tautog's tough mouth and to horse the fish away from obstructions. Tautog feed mainly on shellfish, so the standard baits include crabs, shrimp, clams and sea worms.

FISHING SYSTEMS: Still Fishing.

Cunner

Tautogolabrus adspersus

DESCRIPTION: Similar to the closely related Tautog in outline, except that the mouth is more pointed. Color varies widely from rusty to nearly black. Distinguishable from juvenile Tautog by the gill cover, which is scaled.

SIZE: Usually 6 inches or less; seldom reaches a foot. World record 2 pounds, 3 ounces.

FOOD VALUE: Excellent, but largely ignored because of small size and unwholesome appearance.

GAME QUALITIES: Fun for youngsters, but a bait-stealing nuisance for older anglers seeking larger game.

TACKLE AND BAITS: Handlines, poles and the lightest rods and reels, with tiny hooks baited with worms or clams.

FISHING SYSTEMS: Still Fishing.

OTHER NAMES:
Bergall
Baitstealer

RANGE: *Newfoundland to Chesapeake Bay; most common from Long Island Sound to Maine.*

HABITAT: *Inshore around pilings of docks and piers, and over hard bottom.*

Hogfish
Lachnolaimus maximus

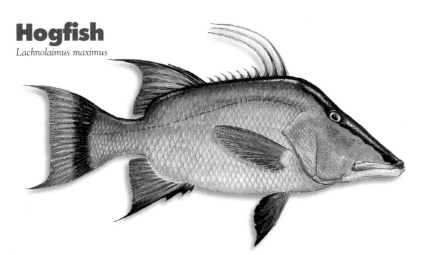

OTHER NAMES:

Hog Snapper

RANGE: *Florida and Bermuda primarily, but reaches Cape Hatteras and has been recorded from New England.*

HABITAT: *Coral reefs and areas of shell or rock bottom.*

DESCRIPTION: Large Hogfish are nothing short of spectacular in appearance, with deep body, long tapering mouth with protruding teeth, a purple band running from the nose to the dorsal and flowing streamers on the dorsal fin's first three rays. Smaller specimens have much the same characteristics but their dorsal streamers are proportionately less regal. Coloration varies, ranging from almost white to soft red.

SIZE: Hogfish larger than 5 pounds are increasingly rare, although an occasional specimen still might top 10 pounds and possibly reach 20 pounds. World record 19 pounds, 8 ounces.

FOOD VALUE: Among the best; very fine-grained, white flesh.

GAME QUALITIES: Big ones put up a good battle initially, but have little stamina.

TACKLE AND BAITS: Light bottom-fishing tackle is best. Spinning and baitcasting gear also are suitable. Shellfish baits are the only really productive offerings—crab, shrimp, squid or scraps of spiny lobster.

FISHING SYSTEMS: Still Fishing.

Puddingwife

Halichoeres radiatus

DESCRIPTION: More slender appearance than the Hogfish, and the color varies from pale green to brilliant green. The head is deep yellow or orange with blue lines. Dark spot at the base of the pectoral fin.

SIZE: A pound or less on average, but sometimes reaches 3 or 4 pounds.

FOOD VALUE: Excellent, but not often eaten.

GAME QUALITIES: Mediocre battler.

TACKLE AND BAIT: Spinning tackle with small hooks and bits of shrimp or cut squid will take Puddingwife. Most catches, however, are made incidentally by reef and bottom fishermen using much heavier gear.

FISHING SYSTEMS: Still Fishing.

OTHER NAMES:

Green Wrasse
Doncella

RANGE: *Most often seen in South Florida and Bermuda, but reaches Cape Hatteras.*

HABITAT: *Coral reefs; also hard bottom with scattered shell.*

Porgies are many and varied in our waters. They seldom get the respect they deserve, but they cooperate heartily with anglers in virtually all settings, from the shoreline out to the deep banks and reefs. Moreover they have provided countless tasty fish dinners following trips where more glamorous types of fish refused to cooperate. Inshore, the Scup and Sheepshead are perhaps the most sought-after Porgies. Offshore partyboat fishermen make hay principally with the Red Porgy, Jolthead Porgy and Whitebone Porgy, depending on the area fished. The Pinfish heads a list of panfish-size Porgies that seem always ready to bite a youngster's hook from dock, seawall or pier.

Chapter

9

The Porgies

Grass Porgy

Calamus arctifrons

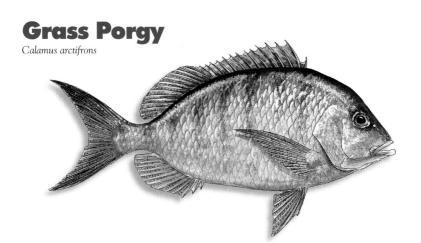

OTHER NAMES:

Grass Bream

RANGE: *South Florida.*

HABITAT: *Nearly always found on grassy bottom in up to 30 feet of water.*

DESCRIPTION: Silvery sides with dark blotches over sides, fins and tail, give this Porgy a camouflaged appearance that hides it well in grass. A vertical bar runs through the eye.

SIZE: Averages around 1 pound; sometimes hits 2 pounds.

FOOD VALUE: Good.

GAME QUALITIES: Quite strong for its size.

TACKLE AND BAITS: Most are caught by anglers fishing inshore shallows for Snapper or Seatrout. Light spinning and baitcasting tackle, with live or dead shrimp and various cutbaits, does the job well.

FISHING SYSTEMS: Still Fishing; Drifting.

Jolthead Porgy

Calamus bajonado

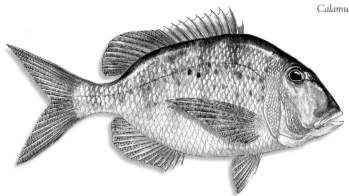

DESCRIPTION: In keeping with its name, the head is more sharply sloped than that of most other Porgies. The usual color is silvery with blue highlights, but the fish may be more brownish when hooked over dark bottom.

SIZE: One of the Atlantic Coast's largest Porgies, it averages a couple of pounds, is fairly common to 5 pounds or more, and can exceed 20 pounds in rare instances. World record 23 pounds, 4 ounces.

FOOD VALUE: Very good.

GAME QUALITIES: Unspectacular but strong.

TACKLE AND BAITS: Light spinning and baitcasting outfits, with nearly any sort of cut fish, shrimp or squid. Again, heavy tackle is the norm on boats fishing offshore waters.

FISHING SYSTEMS: Still Fishing; Drifting.

OTHER NAMES:

Bajonado

RANGE: *Florida to Cape Cod.*

HABITAT: *Over most of its range it is found on offshore reefs or banks, but roams to deep inshore patches off South Florida.*

Knobbed Porgy

Calamus nodosus

OTHER NAMES:

Key West Porgy

RANGE: Florida to Virginia.

HABITAT: Likes deep water, up to 100 feet or so, over coral or rock reefs, or patchy bottom.

DESCRIPTION: A colorful fellow with sloped head, purple or blue face and reddish trim.

SIZE: Common up to 4 pounds; occasionally larger.

FOOD VALUE: Excellent.

GAME QUALITIES: Resistance is very strong for a while, but the outcome seldom is in doubt.

TACKLE AND BAITS: This is a common partyboat catch over most of its range, mixing (for lucky fishermen) with Grouper, Snapper or Sea Bass. The usual gear, therefore, is a pretty heavy boat outfit. Stout baitcasting or spinning outfits are better suited to the task, however. Cut pieces of fish or squid are preferred baits.

FISHING SYSTEMS: Still Fishing; Drifting.

Pinfish

Lagodon rhomboides

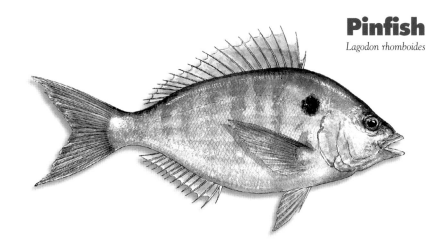

DESCRIPTION: Sharp spines of dorsal and anal fins give this fish its name. The background color is silvery with narrow longitudinal yellow lines and, sometimes, dim vertical bars. There is a dark patch on the lateral line just behind gill cover.

SIZE: Most run 3-6 inches, but a few reach 1 pound or slightly more. World record 3 pounds, 5 ounces.

FOOD VALUE: Not a bad panfish, although quite bony. The rare big ones are as good as other Porgies.

GAME QUALITIES: A hard striker and active little fighter. Fun to catch on very light tackle, especially for youngsters.

TACKLE AND BAITS: Generally, Pinfish are targeted only by adults seeking live bait, or by kids and novices seeking something to catch. Bits of cut shrimp, fish, or bacon, fished on tiny hooks with canepoles or spinning outfits, will pile up the best numbers, but Pinfish are game little fellows that will hit tiny jigs presented with ultralight spinning outfits, or panfish-size flies on a little fly rod.

FISHING SYSTEMS: Drifting; Still Fishing.

OTHER NAMES:
Shiner
Spanish Porgy

RANGE: Florida to Cape Cod; also Bermuda.

HABITAT: In warm seasons, small pinfish swarm over inshore grassflats, or around such cover as rocks, bars and docks. The biggest individuals apparently prefer deeper inshore holes and channels.

Red Porgy

Pagrus pagrus

OTHER NAMES:

Pink Porgy

RANGE: *Florida to New York; straggles farther north.*

HABITAT: *Offshore waters to 500 feet deep or more. In South Florida they stick to the deepest habitat and are seldom caught by anglers. From North Florida to the Mid-Atlantic states, however, they are among the most common partyboat catches in about 50 to 150 feet of water.*

DESCRIPTION: Color ranges from shiny lavender to pink or light red. There are blue spots on the sides and blue lines around the eyes.

SIZE: The most common size is 2 to 3 pounds. Fish to 6 pounds are not rare and the potential is more than 10 pounds. World record 17 pounds.

FOOD VALUE: Excellent.

GAME QUALITIES: Pretty good fighter, though usually overpowered.

TACKLE AND BAITS: Heavy boat rods are most often used—and necessary—because large sinkers are needed. Jut about any sort of bait will attract a Red Porgy, but the most popular are cut fish and cut squid.

FISHING SYSTEMS: Drifting; Still Fishing.

Saucereye Porgy

Calamus calamus

DESCRIPTION: The Porgies are often tough to distinguish, due to similarity of shape and, often, of color too. The Saucereye's name is derived from a blue line below the eye that causes the eye to appear larger. The area between the eyes and mouth is also blue, with overlying gold spots. Body color is silvery.

SIZE: Common at 2-3 pounds; reaches perhaps 7 or 8.

FOOD VALUE: Very good.

GAME QUALITIES: A strong puller.

TACKLE AND BAITS: Same as for the other Porgies described. They bite cooperatively on all the popular dead baits and are usually cranked up by outfits too heavy for much sport. With lighter gear, however, they are not only tasty but sporty.

FISHING SYSTEMS: Still Fishing; Drifting.

OTHER NAMES:
Big-eye Porgy

RANGE: *Florida to Virginia.*

HABITAT: *Usually in fairly deep water, up to 100 feet.*

Scup
Stenotomus chrysops

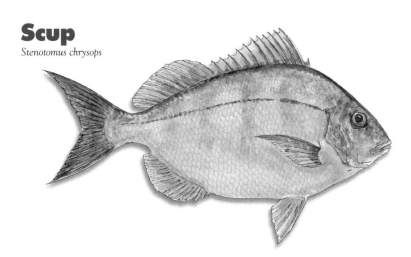

OTHER NAMES:

Northern Porgy

RANGE: *Cape Hatteras to Nova Scotia; straggles a bit farther south.*

HABITAT: *Anglers catch most of their Scup in bays and other protected waters, from docks and piers as well as small boats. Scup, however, are also common in deeper waters of the continental shelf. They prefer hard or rocky bottom.*

DESCRIPTION: Color is dull silver with light or indistinct dark vertical bars on the sides and a blue stripe along the dorsal fin. Bars may be absent on Scup taken over sandy bottom. Tail is forked.

SIZE: Most run 1 to 2 pounds, with a maximum of about 4 pounds. World record 4 pounds, 9 ounces.

FOOD VALUE: Very tasty.

GAME QUALITIES: Pretty scrappy on light tackle, but most of the Scup's great popularity derives from its willingness to bite almost any bait at any time.

TACKLE AND BAITS: Light saltwater outfits are often used, especially when rather heavy sinkers are needed. Baitcasting and spinning gear are entirely adequate as well. Clams, squid, crabs, marine worms and shrimp are the most commonly used natural baits. Few anglers try lures, but Scup will go for small jigs worked slowly on bottom. Chumming with any combination of the baits named—chopped or ground—often leads to large catches.

FISHING SYSTEMS: Still Fishing.

Sea Bream

Archosargus rhomboidalis

DESCRIPTION: Deeper of body than the Pinfish and of larger average size, the Sea Bream is silvery with numerous yellow stripes that give it a golden sheen.

SIZE: Average is 8-12 inches; maximum about 14 inches.

FOOD VALUE: Good.

GAME QUALITIES: A cooperative biter and good tussler.

TACKLE AND BAITS: Light spinning and baitcasting outfits, but preferably with long and rather whippy rods so that long casts can be made in surf and around jetties. Live or dead shrimp and cut fish or squid make good baits. Will hit jigs and other small artificial lures.

FISHING SYSTEMS: Drifting; Still Fishing.

OTHER NAMES:
Golden Pinfish
Golden Shiner

RANGE: Florida to New York.

HABITAT: Common around jetties, and around rocky areas of surf and shorelines. Prefers hard bottom to mud or grass.

Sheepshead
Archosargus probatocephalus

OTHER NAMES:

Sheephead
Convict Fish
Baitstealer

RANGE: *Florida to New York, straggling to Nova Scotia.*

HABITAT: *Mostly bays and protected coastal waterways — even far up brackish and freshwater streams — but also inhabits inshore reefs. Sticks mostly to rock or shell bottom. Loves dock and bridge pilings, artificial reefs and any other structure that wears barnacles. Forages for crustaceans, at times, on shallow soft-bottom flats in the manner of Redfish or Bonefish.*

DESCRIPTION: A mouthful of massive, protruding teeth, resembling those of a sheep, give the fish its name—and also distinguish it from the juvenile Black Drum, which is the only fish likely to cause confusion. Seven vertical black stripes stand out against a dull white, gray or yellowish background. Spines of the dorsal and anal fins are heavy and sharp.

SIZE: Common from 1 pound to about 7 pounds. Individuals exceeding 10 pounds are not rare. The maximum is more than 20 pounds. World record 21 pounds, 4 ounces.

FOOD VALUE: Excellent, thanks largely to its strict diet of shellfish.

GAME QUALITIES: Very challenging on light tackle. Pulls hard, dives hard, and uses is flattened shape to great advantage.

TACKLE AND BAITS: Nothing beats a crustacean bait for luring Sheepshead. Any sort of small crab (fiddler crabs are the traditional favorite), or pieces of large crab, top the menu, but shrimp are usually acceptable, either live or dead. Mollusks such as clams and oysters are also on the menu, as are marine worms. Spinning, baitcasting and light saltwater boat rods deliver the best sport, but rodtips should not be too soft, as the tough and toothy mouth makes it hard to set a hook. Sheepshead will readily hit slow-moving jigs tipped with these baits and, occasionally, will take the bare jig.

FISHING METHODS: Still Fishing.

Silver Porgy

Diplodus argenteus

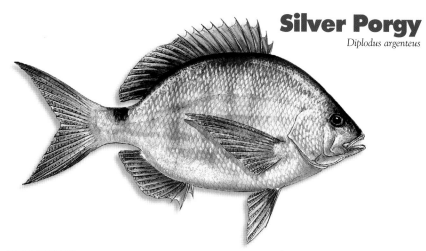

DESCRIPTION: Like the Spottail Pinfish, this species has a dark spot on the caudal peduncle, but the spot is lighter and smaller, usually not extending below the lateral line. This fish is also lighter in overall color and has thin yellowish stripes and dark vertical bars.

SIZE: Averages 6-8 inches; rarely exceeds a pound.

FOOD VALUE: Tasty but, again, the bones can be troublesome.

GAME QUALITIES: Zippy fighter and strong for its size.

TACKLE AND BAITS: Canepoles or light spinning tackle, with bits of cut fish or shellfish as bait.

FISHING SYSTEMS: Still Fishing; Drifting.

OTHER NAMES:
Spot Porgy

RANGE: *A tropical Porgy, largely confined to Florida.*

HABITAT: *Likes reefs or rocks in clear, shallow water.*

Spottail Pinfish

Diplodus holbrooki

OTHER NAMES:

Spot Porgy

RANGE: Florida to New Jersey.

HABITAT: Generally likes deeper water than the Pinfish, but the two often are represented in mixed catches from the shallows.

DESCRIPTION: The name refers to a large black patch on the caudal peduncle. The shape is more round than that of the Pinfish. Color is brownish above, silvery below.

SIZE: Can grow to a pound or more, but usually runs 6 to 8 inches.

FOOD VALUE: Being somewhat larger on average, it is more attractive as a meal than the Pinfish, although both are tasty.

GAME QUALITIES: A scrappy fighter for its size.

TACKLE AND BAITS: Top choice would be a light or ultralight spinning outfit with very small hook and cut fish, shrimp or squid for bait.

FISHING SYSTEMS: Still Fishing; Drifting.

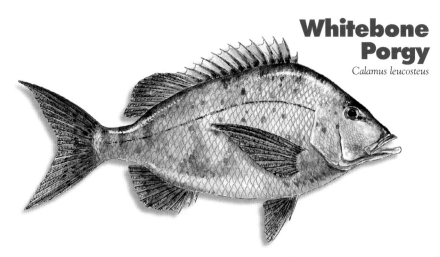

Whitebone Porgy
Calamus leucosteus

DESCRIPTION: Dark blotches and scattered yellow dots help identify this Porgy. Overall color is a silvery white, with blue lines on the head.

SIZE: Frequently runs to 4 pounds and sometimes larger.

FOOD VALUE: Very good; large enough for bones along the centerline of the fillet to be easily trimmed out.

GAME QUALITIES: Nearly as tough as Snappers of similar size.

TACKLE AND BAITS: As with other deepwater Porgies, most are caught by anglers seeking more prestigious fish such as Grouper with heavy bottom-fishing outfits. Lighter ocean gear, or heavy baitcasting and spinning outfits are much to be preferred, however. Cut pieces of fish or squid, or small baitfish (live or dead), are productive baits.

FISHING SYSTEMS: Still Fishing; Drifting.

OTHER NAMES:
White Porgy
Silver Snapper

RANGE: *Florida to Virginia.*

HABITAT: *Rocks, reefs and patchy bottom up to 100 feet or more.*

This huge family may well provide more sport for more Atlantic Coast anglers than any other group. In its particular size class, every one of its members is a top-notch gamester, and one or more of the clan is available to any fishermen, whether he tosses his bait from a shoreline structure, or from an offshore boat. The Giant Bluefin Tuna ranks right alongside the Blue Marlin and Swordfish as a premier big-game fish, with its relatives—the Yellowfin and Bigeye Tunas—not far behind. Among the Mackerels, the King and the Wahoo are middleweight pets of offshore anglers—especially the King, which is a huge favorite of the small-boat fleet in the South. On the dark side, however, many of the Tunas and Mackerels are also commercially valuable, overexploited and heavily regulated, so be sure to check federal, state and provincial regulations before going after them.

Tunas and Mackerels

Albacore

Atlantic Bonito

Bigeye Tuna

Bluefin Tuna

Little Tunny

Skipjack Tuna

Yellowfin Tuna

Atlantic Mackerel

Cero

Chub Mackerel

Frigate Mackerel

King Mackerel

Spanish Mackerel

Wahoo

Albacore

Thunnus alalunga

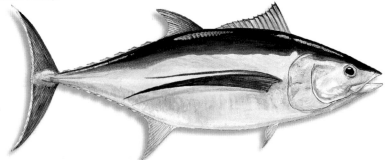

OTHER NAMES:

Longfin Tuna

RANGE: Central Florida to Nova Scotia.

HABITAT: The open sea. Stays deep in southern waters, but may roam near the surface in summer in the northern end of its range.

DESCRIPTION: This is one of the easiest Tunas to identify, thanks to its extra-long pectoral fins, and also because the trailing edge of the tail is white. Color is dark blue above, white below, with no markings.

SIZE: Usually 10-50 pounds; sometimes exceeds 80 pounds. World record 88 pounds, 2 ounces.

FOOD VALUE: White, relatively tasteless flesh makes it less of a treat than other Tunas, although its blandness is preferred by most people who buy their Tuna in cans.

GAME QUALITIES: Pound for pound a standout — even among its hard-fighting relatives.

TACKLE AND BAITS: Difficult to target in most areas, it can be caught by trolling small offshore lures, feathers, spoons and small rigged baits such as Ballyhoo or strips.

FISHING METHODS: Trolling.

Atlantic Bonito

Sarda Sarda

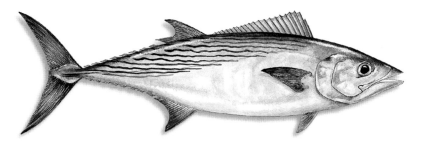

DESCRIPTION: Differs from Little Tunny in having a series of wavy lines along upper half of body, and no spots on lower half. Additionally, its two dorsal fins are not divided.

SIZE: The average is about 4-10 pounds, and the maximum perhaps 20 pounds. World record 18 pounds, 4 ounces.

FOOD VALUE: Another dark-meat variety that is not well regarded but good.

SPORTING QUALITIES: Like other Tunas, an excellent fighter.

TACKLE AND BAITS: Usually overmatched with ocean trolling gear, but a great target, when the opportunity arises, for light casting tackle. Eagerly hits spoons, jigs and streamer flies, and also live fish and strip baits.

FISHING SYSTEMS: Trolling; Drifting; Casting.

OTHER NAMES:

Common Bonito
Northern Bonito

RANGE: *Cape Cod to North Florida; straggling northward to Nova Scotia and southward to South Florida. Prefers temperate waters to tropical.*

HABITAT: *The open sea, but roams to the beaches.*

Bigeye Tuna

Thunnus obesus

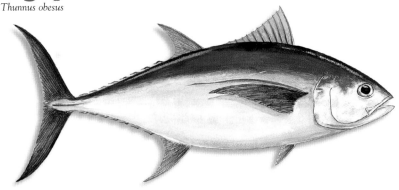

RANGE: *Maine to South Florida; also Bermuda.*

HABITAT: *The open sea. As the big eye indicates, it stays deep most of the time and so may not be as rare as the low number of angling encounters would seem to indicate.*

DESCRIPTION: Similar to the Yellowfin at a glance, but the gold stripe common to the Yellowfin is very dim or absent. The eye is indeed larger, but this might not be readily apparent without a side-by-side comparison. The first dorsal fin is yellow and the finlets are yellow with black edges.

SIZE: Runs to about the same sizes as the Yellowfin Tuna—from a few pounds to a maximum of 400 or slightly more. World record 392 pounds, 6 ounces.

FOOD VALUE: Excellent.

GAME QUALITIES: Among the strongest and most rugged of fighters.

TACKLE AND BAITS: Seldom targeted, it is usually caught while chunking or chumming for other large Tunas, or by deep trolling.

FISHING SYSTEMS: Trolling; Drifting; Still Fishing.

Blackfin Tuna

Thunnus atlanticus

DESCRIPTION: Color is dark overall, with a bronze stripe down the side that can cause confusion with the more golden stripe of the Yellowfin Tuna. The finlets, however, are dark with white edges.

SIZE: Common from 2 to 20 pounds; exceeds 40 pounds. World record 45 pounds, 8 ounces.

FOOD VALUE: Excellent.

GAME QUALITIES: Among the best of fighters, relative to size.

TACKLE AND BAITS: Light classes of ocean tackle, plus spinning and baitcasting outfits. For trolling, choose small offshore lures, feathers, spoons and small rigged baits such as Ballyhoo or strips. Blackfins can be spooky and so trolling baits often must be pulled far astern. Like Yellowfin Tuna, they can be chummed with live Pilchards, Anchovies or other small baitfish, and fished for with the same bait, or by casting. Best hard lures are white jigs, tied with bucktail or feathers to provide a larger profile. Flies should be similarly tied—to imitate size and color of the live chum.

FISHING SYSTEMS: Trolling; Drifting; Still Fishing.

OTHER NAMES:

Bermuda Tuna
Football

RANGE: *Cape Cod to South Florida; also Bermuda.*

HABITAT: *The open sea.*

Bluefin Tuna

Thunnus thynnus

OTHER NAMES:

Giant Tuna
Horse Mackerel

RANGE: *Entire Atlantic Coast from South Florida to Newfoundland, but common only from the Carolinas northward; also Bermuda.*

HABITAT: *From the deep sea to near shore in northern areas.*

DESCRIPTION: The stout body is dark blue above, shading to yellowish on the sides and silver below. All fins and finlets are steely blue.

SIZE: From small schooling fish of a few pounds (often called "footballs") all the way up to giants that average well over 500 pounds and sometimes exceed a half-ton. World record 1,496 pounds.

FOOD VALUE: Excellent.

GAME QUALITIES: A Giant Bluefin lacks the showiness of Swordfish and Marlin but is rated the toughest of all fish to fight and land. It has strength, stamina and speed in boundless quantity.

TACKLE AND BAITS: Ocean tackle scaled to the expected size of the fish. Only the heaviest sporting outfits with lines testing 80 or 130 pounds are adequate for the giants. A variety of trolling lures, such as feathers, cedar plugs and offshore trolling lures are used for school Tuna. Giants will hit the same trolling baits but preferably in larger sizes. Rigged natural baits, such as large Mackerel, are also effective for trolling, either alone or in combination with a feather or other lure. All sizes of Bluefins respond readily to "chunking," and this is the standard approach in many areas and seasons. Chunking can be described as the restrained dispensing of large pieces of Butterfish, Herring or other baitfish, rather than ground chum, to attract the Tuna. In this approach, the hooks are usually baited with whole fish of the same type used in the chunking.

FISHING SYSTEMS: Trolling; Drifting; Still Fishing.

Little Tunny

Euthynnus alletteratus

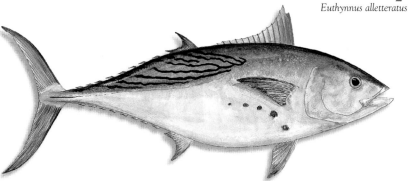

DESCRIPTION: Color is rich blue above, silvery below, with wavy patterns on the upper side, aft of the dorsal fin, and spots around the pectoral fin.

SIZE: Common in various sizes from less than a pound to 10 or 15 pounds; occasionally exceeds 30 pounds. World record 35 pounds, 2 ounces.

FOOD VALUE: Not highly valued by most, but very good especially if the darker meat is trimmed away.

GAME QUALITIES: Another outstanding battler that struggles long and stubbornly on light tackle. Unfortunately, many are caught on heavier gear by anglers seeking bigger game.

TACKLE AND BAITS: Schools can often be approached and cast to with jigs, spoons and small plugs. They can be moody and selective, however, so you may have to try various baits and retrieves. This also is a great target for fly casters, and a rather common catch for anglers on ocean piers, who usually get them on small live baits. Trollers take them on everything from offshore lures and rigged Ballyhoo or Cigar Minnows to small feathers.

FISHING SYSTEMS: Drifting; Trolling; Casting.

OTHER NAMES:

Florida Bonito
False Albacore

RANGE: South Florida to Cape Cod; more numerous in southern waters.

HABITAT: A roamer, from close inshore to the deep sea.

Skipjack Tuna

Katsuwonus pelamis

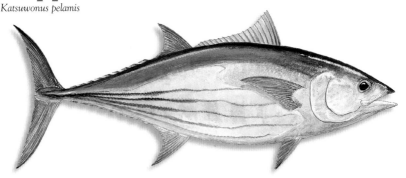

OTHER NAMES:

Striped Tuna
Oceanic Bonito
Arctic Bonito

RANGE: *South Florida to Cape Cod, straggling to Nova Scotia.*

HABITAT: *The deep sea.*

DESCRIPTION: Horizontal stripes on lower half of body distinguishes it from others of its clan.

SIZE: Runs in schools of similar-size fish, usually 2-10 pounds, but often exceeding 15 pounds and sometimes surpassing 30 pounds. World record 45 pounds, 4 ounces.

FOOD VALUE: The flesh is very dark and not to most tastes, but very good and nutritious.

GAME QUALITIES: A terrific light-tackle battler.

TACKLE AND BAITS: Large schools are common at the surface and provide fine targets for casters tossing small jigs, plugs and flies. Trollers also score heavily with light tackle classes of trolling tackle and small feathers, spoons and trolling lures.

FISHING SYSTEMS: Trolling; Drifting.

Yellowfin Tuna

Thunnus albacares

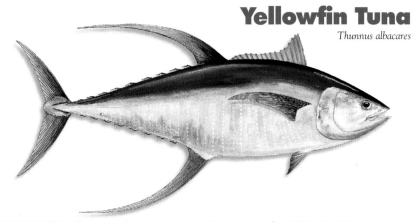

DESCRIPTION: The second dorsal and anal fins of very large individuals are elongated and lunate—a feature not found on any other Tuna—but small Yellowfins lack this trademark and are difficult to distinguish from Bigeye and Blackfin Tunas of similar size. Finlets of the Yellowfin are yellow, trimmed in black. A gold stripe runs along the upper side, and the light underside usually shows spots and/or wavy lines.

SIZE: Schools of like-size fish may range anywhere from a few pounds to 50 or 100 pounds. Individuals up to 300 pounds are reasonably common, and the maximum is perhaps 400 pounds. World record 388 pounds, 12 ounces.

FOOD VALUE: One of the best.

GAME QUALITIES: Equal to Bluefin Tuna in similar size categories.

TACKLE AND BAITS: For bigger fish, ocean outfits with lines testing 50 or 80 pounds are not overpowering. Lighter line classes—20 and 30—can also be used effectively in experienced hands, even for fish over 100 pounds. Most are probably caught trolling with offshore trolling lures or rigged baits, but in many areas the best approach is to anchor on a reef near deep blue water and bring in the fish by chumming liberally with small baitfish such as Anchovies or Pilchards, or by chunking. When responding to chum, Yellowfins can often be hooked by casting artificial lures with spinning, baitcasting or heavy fly tackle—and landed, too, if the angler has enough line on his spool, plus a lot of patience and a little luck.

FISHING SYSTEMS: Trolling; Still Fishing; Drifting.

OTHER NAMES:

Allison Tuna
Ahi

RANGE: *New England to South Florida; also Bermuda.*

HABITAT: *The open sea; frequently found near reef dropoffs and canyon edges.*

Atlantic Mackerel

Scomber scombrus

OTHER NAMES:

**Tinker Mackerel
Northern Mackerel**

RANGE: The Canadian
Maritimes to Cape Hatteras;
occasionally to South Carolina
and Georgia.

HABITAT: Open water from the
deep sea all the way to shore,
and also large bays.

DESCRIPTION: The back is dark blue or green. For the full length of the body, the sides are marked with vertical, wavy lines that extend to, or just below, the lateral line. Belly is white; tail forked; mouth large with no prominent teeth.

SIZE: Averages a foot in length, but sometimes run to 18 inches. Specimens over 5 pounds have been reported, but 2-pounders are uncommon. World record 2 pounds, 10 ounces.

FOOD VALUE: Depends on personal taste. Oily, but very good to many people. Widely sold in salted form.

GAME QUALITIES: A spirited little fighter when taken on suitably light tackle.

TACKLE AND BAITS: Nothing can beat light and ultra-light spinning outfits, or light fly rods. Mackerel are ravenous feeders on shrimp, crabs and other invertebrates, as well as small baitfish, so they will accept a great variety of artificial lures—especially when thickly schooled. Small, bright spoons and metal squids are always good, as are small streamer flies tied with Mylar or other glitter. Jigs and swimming plugs are other choices.

FISHING SYSTEMS: Trolling; Casting.

Cero

Scomberomorus regalis

DESCRIPTION: Here's another fish that can be confused with the Spanish Mackerel. The Cero, however, often has both gold and black markings, and some of the marks take the form of a broken line running down the center of the side from the pectoral fin to the caudal.

SIZE: Averages about the same as the Spanish, 1-5 pounds, but 10-pounders are far more common and the maximum approaches 20 pounds. World record 17 pounds, 2 ounces.

FOOD VALUE: Very good. Lighter flesh than the Spanish Mackerel, but nearly as oily.

GAME QUALITIES: A vicious striker and good battler. Long, speedy runs are its main features. Sometimes clears the surface when it strikes, but does not leap after being hooked.

TACKLE AND BAITS: Light trolling gear, along with spinning, baitcasting and fly outfits. As when seeking Spanish Mackerel, spinning is often best because of its fast pickup. Spoons are perhaps the best trolling lures. For casting, try silver spoons or nylon and bucktail jigs. Flies that work best are those tied with Mylar or other flashy material. Best natural baits are Ballyhoo and any small, silvery baitfish. Strips and live shrimp work too, but not nearly so well.

FISHING SYSTEMS: Drifting; Trolling; Still Fishing; Casting.

OTHER NAMES:

Painted Mackerel

RANGE: *Although it has been caught along the entire Atlantic Coast as far north as Cape Cod, the Cero is basically a tropical fish and far more plentiful in South Florida than anywhere farther north. Also found in Bermuda.*

HABITAT: *Coral reefs and inshore patches and shoals. Ventures to deep blue water as well.*

Chub Mackerel

Scomber japonicus

OTHER NAMES:

**Tinker Mackerel
Hardhead**

RANGE: *Florida to Nova Scotia. Far more common north of Cape Hatteras.*

HABITAT: *Largely coastal, but occurs both offshore and in large bays.*

DESCRIPTION: Superficially similar to the Atlantic Mackerel, but the wavy lines are fewer and lighter, and there also are markings below the lateral line.

SIZE: Averages less than a foot long; occasionally to 15 inches. World record 4 pounds, 12 ounces.

FOOD VALUE: Good but oily.

GAME QUALITIES: Hard striker and fast runner. Good fight on very light spinning lines.

TACKLE AND BAITS: Like the Northern Mackerel, the Chub is not picky about its diet. Small minnows, strip baits and shrimp are always good, as are tiny jigs and flies.

FISHING SYSTEMS: Trolling; Casting.

Frigate Mackerel

Auxis thazard

OTHER NAMES:

**Bonito
Frigate Tuna**

RANGE: *One or both species occur along the entire Atlantic Coast.*

HABITAT: *The open sea, but often near deeper reefs.*

DESCRIPTION: Looks much like the Little Tunny, with the same wavy lines on dorsal area, and dots under pectoral fin. The dorsal fins are widely separated. A similar species is the **Bullet Mackerel, *Auxis rochei,*** but without dots.

SIZE: Averages a foot; rarely reaches two feet. World record 3 pounds, 12 ounces.

FOOD VALUE: Poor by most tastes. Dark and oily.

GAME QUALITIES: Tough but too small to do much.

TACKLE AND BAITS: Often fished for as bait for larger fish with spinning outfits and small spoons or jigs.

FISHING SYSTEMS: Trolling; Casting.

King Mackerel

Scomberomorus cavalla

DESCRIPTION: Elongated, heavy body is greenish above but mostly silvery and unmarked, except in juveniles. The mouth is large and fitted with razor-sharp teeth. Juveniles have pale spots and may be confused with the Spanish Mackerel, but their bodies are slimmer. The lateral line dips sharply.

SIZE: In large schools, the average size may run from a couple of pounds to about 20. Big fish, running from 30 to 50 pounds or more, are not schoolers but may gang up. Potential maximum size is possibly 100. World record 93 pounds.

FOOD VALUE: Rich flesh fine broiled or smoked.

GAME QUALITIES: Kings are strong and sizzling fighters, making use of both speed and strength.

TACKLE AND BAITS: The most popular gear is light to medium ocean tackle with lines testing from 20-40 pounds, but Kings of all sizes can be caught on spinning, baitcasting and even fly tackle. Surf tackle is the best choice for pier fishing. Spoons trolled behind planers are good, as are rigged Cigar Minnows and feather-minnow combinations. King Mackerel respond well to chum, particularly chum containing ground Menhaden (Bunker) or Menhaden oil. Fishing with live Menhaden, Herring, Cigar Minnows or Sardines is probably the most productive system of all, but drifting with rigged baits, strips or live shrimp can be effective too.

FISHING SYSTEMS: Drifting; Trolling; Still Fishing; Casting.

OTHER NAMES:

Kingfish
King

RANGE: *South Florida to North Carolina; straggles to New England.*

HABITAT: *Widely distributed in coastal waters out to the edge of the continental shelf, but greatest concentrations are found fairly close to shore—and even right along the ocean beaches. Some of the biggest fish, in fact, are often taken from piers, or from boats working close to the beach, and are sometimes referred to as "Beachrunners." Twice-yearly runs occur in South Florida. The season off North Florida, Georgia and the Carolinas runs from spring to fall.*

Spanish Mackerel

Scomberomorus maculatus

Mack
Spanish

RANGE: *Florida to Chesapeake Bay, sometimes roaming father north — even to Cape Cod — in late summer.*

HABITAT: *Largely coastal, but invades bays and rivers and is also found offshore at times.*

DESCRIPTION: The body of an adult is rather deep, with dark back and silvery sides. There are many vivid yellow spots on the side. The body is proportionately deeper than that of a juvenile King mackerel, but if in doubt, the only true identifier is the lateral line, which tapers rather gently from front to back with no severe dip.

SIZE: Usually I to 5 pounds, but 7-pounders are taken now and then, and the potential is to 10 or slightly more. World record 13 pounds.

FOOD VALUE: Very good if fresh. Fillets are rich and oily.

GAME QUALITIES: Battle features lightning runs on light tackle, and there may be several of them. Also resists stubbornly at boatside.

TACKLE AND BAITS: Light tackle provides great sport with Spanish. Spinning, baitcasting and fly outfits are all widely used but spinning is best because the faster retrieve of a spinning reel is sometimes needed to move a lure fast enough to attract the speedy Mackerel. Best lures are small white nylon jigs and silver spoons, but many others work, including topwaters at times. Flies should be small with lots of flash. Best baits are small silvery baitfish, live shrimp and drifted strips.

FISHING SYSTEMS: Drifting; Trolling; Still Fishing; Casting.

Wahoo

Acanthocybium solanderi

DESCRIPTION: A live or fresh-caught Wahoo would be difficult to mistake, with its long, slender body, vivid zebra-like stripes of white and deep blue or black, and a narrow, elongated mouth equipped with razor-sharp teeth.

SIZE: Most catches run 20-50 pounds, but individuals pushing 100 pounds are not too rare. The potential is to 150 or more. World record 158 pounds, 8 ounces.

FOOD VALUE: The flesh is rather dry but white and mild. Excellent smoked.

GAME QUALITIES: One of the fastest of all gamefish, the Wahoo's fight features speed, usually in the form of several dazzling runs. The Wahoo may strike a surface bait in spectacular, greyhounding fashion, but seldom jumps after being hooked.

TACKLE AND BAITS: Surface trolling is sometimes effective, but deep trolling is much more likely to produce a Wahoo. Unfortunately, many are hooked on heavy tackle, incidentally to Billfishing, but the best tackle choices are light to medium ocean trolling outfits with lines up to 30-pound test. Even 50-pound isn't too heavy for good sport with big specimens. A few have been caught by deepjigging or ocean casting with spinning and baitcasting tackle—even fly tackle on rare occasion. Most productive trolling lure is a weighted feather, rigged in combination with a whole small baitfish or large strip.

FISHING SYSTEMS: Trolling; Drifting.

OTHER NAMES:

Peto
Ono

RANGE: *New York and Middle Atlantic states to Florida; also Bermuda.*

HABITAT: *Deep blue water, especially around rips, weedlines, seamounts and other favorable feeding locations.*

Great size, blazing speed and spectacular jumping ability. With resumes like that, who can deny that Marlin, Swordfish and Sailfish rule the offshore sportfishing arena? Two of our Billfishes — the Blue Marlin and Swordfish — rank among the largest fish in the Atlantic. The White Marlin, Sailfish and Longbill Spearfish are lightweights by comparison, but are even more acrobatic than their larger cousins and are equally difficult to conquer on tackle that is scaled for them. One of the Billfishes listed in this chapter — the Hatchet Marlin — is something of a mystery. Although several catches of this exceedingly rare fish have been authenticated from Florida, scientists are still uncertain as to whether the Hatchet Marlin is a new type or simply a variant form of the White.

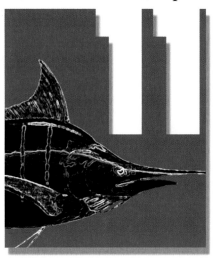

The Billfishes

Blue Marlin

Hatchet Marlin

Longbill Spearfish

Sailfish

Swordfish

White Marlin

Blue Marlin

Makaira nigricans

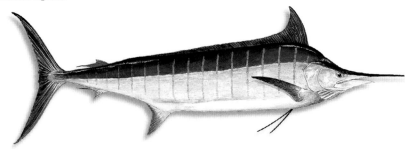

OTHER NAMES:

Aguja azul

RANGE: *South Florida to Nova Scotia; also Bermuda.*

HABITAT: *The deep sea. The most appealing areas to fish are around offshore rips, seamounts, canyon edges and in the vicinity of schooling forage fish, such as Tuna and Dolphin.*

DESCRIPTION: The most common color is dark blue, almost black on the dorsal surface and upper sides, shading to white on the lower portions of the body. Usually, several vertical stripes are noticeable, and sometimes these are quite vivid. Coloration varies a great deal. Size alone is often the obvious identifying feature, but confusion can arise when comparing juvenile Blue Marlin to White Marlin, Spearfish and the illusory Hatchet Marlin. The feature that distinguishes the Blue from the White and Hatchet Marlins is the pointed dorsal fin that curves sharply downward.

SIZE: Commonly up to 500 pounds and a rare few going over 1,000 pounds. World record (Atlantic) 1,402 pounds, 2 ounces.

FOOD VALUE: Good, but seldom eaten, since anglers generally release their fish.

GAME QUALITIES: Ranks at the top of the list for power, speed and spectacle.

TACKLE AND BAITS: While many Blues have been caught on lighter gear, the logical choice is a balanced ocean trolling outfit in the 50-pound or even 80-pound line class. Marlin baits fall into three categories: artificial trolling lures; live baitfish, such as smaller Tuna or Bonito; and rigged natural baits, such as Mackerel, Bonito, Mullet or large Ballyhoo. Lures allow more area of the ocean to be covered in the search for a hungry Blue. In somewhat limited areas, such as along weedlines or around seamounts and other well-established grounds, live bait is usually preferred. Rigged baits always are a good compromise.

FISHING SYSTEMS: Trolling; sometimes Drifting.

Hatchet Marlin

Tetrapturus ?

DESCRIPTION: Although considered a myth by some, several individuals have been examined by reputable scientists, but they have yet to classify the Hatchet Marlin as a separate species. It may simply be a variant of the White Marlin, but a difference in the scales lends credence to the belief that it might be distinct. The scales are round, whereas those of the other Marlins are pointed. Coloration is similar to the other Marlins, but it is closer to the White than to the Blue in body proportions. The name comes from the dorsal fin, which does not dip in the manner of the Blue and White, but tapers gradually to the rear.

SIZE: Uncertain; possibly to 200 pounds or more.

FOOD VALUE: Untried.

GAME QUALITIES: No doubt the same as a Blue or White of similar size.

TACKLE AND BAITS: Not targetable. Probably takes the full array of billfish baits and lures.

FISHING SYSTEMS: Trolling.

RANGE: The few examples have come mostly from the Gulf of Mexico, but at least one suspected Hatchet Marlin was caught off Florida and others have been reported. If it is truly a separate species, it probably occurs throughout the tropics and warm temperate areas.

HABITAT: The deep sea.

Longbill Spearfish

Tetrapturus pfluegeri

OTHER NAMES:

Atlantic Spearfish

RANGE: *South Florida to New York.*

HABITAT: *The deep sea.*

DESCRIPTION: The bill is actually quite short, compared to that of the Sailfish or White Marlin. The name "Longbill" relates only to other Spearfishes occurring in different areas of the world. Color usually is navy blue above; silvery on the sides and underparts. The dorsal fin is pointed at the front but dips only slightly and remains high for its full length—although not nearly high enough to mistake this species for a Sailfish.

SIZE: Most catches run 20-40 pounds; tops is possibly 100 pounds. World record 127 pounds, 13 ounces.

FOOD VALUE: Probably good but should be released.

GAME QUALITIES: Similar to Sailfish, but seldom as large and more easily handled.

TACKLE AND BAITS: See Sailfish and White Marlin. Spearfish cannot be targeted and most catches are incidental to those fisheries.

FISHING SYSTEMS: Trolling.

Sailfish

Istiophorus platypterus

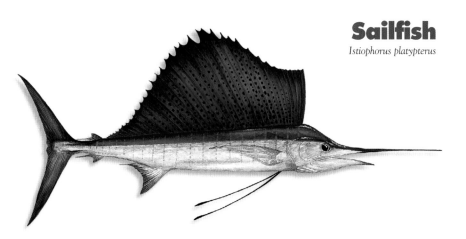

DESCRIPTION: There's no mistaking this Billfish, thanks to its magnificent sail-like dorsal fin, which it often waves above the surface like a cape when chasing baitfish. Color is usually dark blue to black above and silvery below. Vertical stripes often are visible on sides when the fish is alive.

SIZE: Sailfish are caught from less than 10 pounds to more than 100 pounds, with the average being in the area of 35-60 pounds. Potential maximum is less than 150 pounds. World record (Atlantic) 141 pounds, 1 ounce.

FOOD VALUE: Most are released but they are very good broiled or smoked, and should be kept if inadvertently killed.

GAME QUALITIES: Unsurpassed in its size range for combined strength and spectacle.

TACKLE AND BAITS: Light ocean trolling or heavy spinning outfits. Lines testing 12 or 20 pounds are adequate in experienced hands and provide great sport. In Southeast Florida, live-baiting—either by kite fishing or flatline drifting—has become perhaps the most popular approach to sailfishing, with Blue Runners, Goggle-eyes, Pilchards or Pinfish being the common offerings. Historically, most Sailfishing has been done with rigged trolling baits, mainly Ballyhoo and strips of Bonito or other small fish. With a few seasonal exceptions, Sailfish north of Central Florida stay well offshore and are mostly taken by mixed-bag trolling, often with artificial baits.

FISHING SYSTEMS: Trolling; Drifting.

OTHER NAMES:

Sail
Spindlebeak

RANGE: *South Florida to New York, but far more are caught off Florida than elsewhere. Also found in Bermuda.*

HABITAT: *Like other Billfishes, the Sailfish is an ocean species, but in the southern areas it often can be found closer to land than the rest, seeming to prefer the edge of the Gulf Stream, or inside the Stream where coral reefs, ledges and wrecks concentrate bait.*

Swordfish

Xiphias gladius

OTHER NAMES:

Broadbill
Broadbill
  Swordfish

RANGE: *Nova Scotia to South Florida.*

HABITAT: *The deep sea.*

DESCRIPTION: The Broadbill is in a family apart from other billfishes. Its huge bill—or sword—is much longer and wider than the bills of Marlins and Sailfish. The eye is also very large. Color is mostly dark brown to purple, with whitish undersides. It is thick-bodied and powerfully built, with a high, crescent-shaped dorsal fin and broadly forked tail. The pectoral fins are also large and crescent shaped.

SIZE: Although Swordfish can grow to 1,000 pounds and historically have averaged 200 or more, relentless commercial longline fishing lowered the average to under 50 pounds. World record 1,182 pounds.

FOOD VALUE: Unfortunately for the outlook of the species, Swordfish are among the best.

GAME QUALITIES: Although not as aerial-minded as the Blue Marlin, the Swordfish nevertheless is a powerful foe and a spectacular, if not frequent, jumper.

TACKLE AND BAITS: The best Swordfish bait always has been a large, rigged natural squid, but rigged baitfishes work too. During recent decades, many Swordfish as heavy as 400 pounds, and sometimes more, were caught by sportsmen drifting deep baits at night—a system developed and perfected in South Florida, but used with success at other points along the Atlantic Coast. The classic system, practiced principally out of Long Island and New England ports, was pulling rigged baits in front of sighted fish as they "tailed" at the surface.

FISHING SYSTEMS: Drifting; Trolling.

White Marlin

Tetrapturus albidus

DESCRIPTION: Proportionately slimmer than the Blue Marlin, but similarly colored, a White can be distinguished from a small Blue by the rounded tips of dorsal, anal and pectoral fins.

SIZE: Maximum is less than 200 pounds, with most catches ranging from 50 to 100 pounds. World record 181 pounds, 14 ounces.

FOOD VALUE: Good, but commercially protected and seldom eaten by sportsmen.

GAME QUALITIES: Lacks the size and power of a Blue, but on appropriate tackle it is a spectacular jumper and long-distance runner.

TACKLE AND BAITS: Light ocean trolling or heavy spinning outfits with lines up to 30-pound test; 12- and 20-pound lines are tops for sport. Anglers targeting White Marlin usually choose rigged trolling baits, including squid, strips and Ballyhoo. They eagerly strike small live baits, of course, and artificial trolling lures also take many Whites.

FISHING SYSTEMS: Trolling; sometimes Drifting.

OTHER NAMES:

Aguja blanca

RANGE: *South Florida to Nova Scotia; also Bermuda. In terms of dependable fishing numbers it is the most widely distributed of Atlantic billfishes.*

HABITAT: *Like the Blue Marlin, a roamer of the open sea, and sought by anglers wherever feeding conditions or temperatures are most favorable.*

Cod and their relatives — principally the Haddock, Pollock and Hakes — hold roughly the same place in the hearts of bottom fishermen in the North as Grouper and Snapper do in the South. They form the mainstay menu of partyboat fishermen from Canada to Long Island, while also being available, at many times and in many places, to the small-boater as well. Even surf fishermen can get a shot at Cod — provided they are willing to face the Atlantic in dead of winter. Although there is a definite order of desirability, with Scrod (small Cod) at the top the list, all these fish make fine table fare. The dark side to that is that they also head the list of commercial prizes, and their numbers suffer hugely as a result.

The Cods

Atlantic Cod

Gadus morhua

OTHER NAMES:

Scrod
Morue

RANGE: Northern Canada to Virginia, but the heart of Cod Country runs from Newfoundland to New Jersey. The storied Cod grounds are the Grand Banks of Newfoundland and George's Bank offshore of Cape Cod, but many closer grounds off Nova Scotia, the Gulf of Maine, southern New England and Long Island produce good catches for sportsmen.

HABITAT: Mostly found on rock-littered or shell-strewn bottom, the bigger fish stay offshore, as a rule, in at least 50 feet of water, often much more. A few large ones, however, join the small fellows near the coastline off the Canadian Maritimes, New England, New York and New Jersey, especially in fall and winter.

DESCRIPTION: Large head and heavy body with small scales. Tail fin is square. Three dorsal and 2 anal fins. Chin is barbeled. Color varies widely, from light gray to brown or nearly black. Body covered by brown or rusty spots. Lateral line is white.

SIZE: Averages 8-12 pounds, but some reach 60 pounds. Those caught close to shore are generally well under 10 pounds. Historically, Cod exceeding 200 pounds have been recorded, but a fish half that size would be an oddity today. World record 98 pounds, 12 ounces.

FOOD VALUE: So good that its existence continues to be threatened by commercial overfishing. Broiled or sauteed fillets of fish under 5 pounds (Scrod) are the first choice of gourmets.

GAME QUALITIES: Cod are not famous for fight, especially since heavy gear is usually employed, due to depth, current and heavy sinkers.

TACKLE AND BAITS: Stout boat rods, medium-capacity saltwater reels and lines up to 50 or even 80-pound test are usual choices of partyboat fishermen. Lighter gear can be used successfully when it's possible to reach bottom with lighter sinkers, or when jigging. Cod will take many different baits, with the most popular being squid, clams, crab, cut fish or whole small fish.

FISHING SYSTEMS: Still Fishing; Drifting.

Atlantic Tomcod

Microgadus tomcod

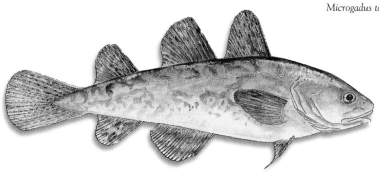

DESCRIPTION: Virtually a small copy of its larger relative, the Tomcod differs in having a rounded tail fin, and slightly rounder first dorsal and anal fins, and mottled markings rather than spots. The usual color is olive or brown on the sides, yellowish below.

SIZE: Up to 12 inches, on average. Tops is about 16 inches.

FOOD VALUE: Excellent.

GAME QUALITIES: Not too active on the end of a line.

TACKLE AND BAITS: Almost anything goes, from handlines to boat rods. Light spinning and baitcasting gear are best suited for sport. All the common baits work well—marine worms, clams, squid and cut fish, to name a few.

FISHING SYSTEMS: Still Fishing; Drifting.

OTHER NAMES:

Tommie

RANGE: *Newfoundland to Virginia.*

HABITAT: *Strictly coastal and roams far up freshwater rivers. Most angling catches are made from jetties, docks, piers and from small boats over hard or rocky bottom in shallow water.*

Haddock

Melanogrammus aeglefinus

RANGE: *Labrador to New York; occasionally south to Virginia in deep offshore waters.*

HABITAT: *Prefers hard bottom and stays offshore, generally in water 100 feet deep or more. Often mixes with Cod in deep water, but seldom ventures near shore.*

DESCRIPTION: Similar in silhouette to the Cod, but the first dorsal fin is high and pointed, and the tail slightly forked. Color is gray above, silvery below, and the lateral line is black — reminiscent of the southern Snook. There is also a black spot, called the "Devil's thumbprint," above the pectoral fin.

SIZE: Usually 2-4 pounds, with a 10-pounder being a real trophy. Rarely reaches 20 or 30 pounds. World record 14 pounds, 15 ounces.

FOOD VALUE: Excellent; considered superior to Cod by most, whether fresh or smoked (Finan Haddie).

GAME QUALITIES: Not a line-breaker.

TACKLE AND BAITS: Usually taken on bottom-fishing tackle by anglers using heavy sinkers and seeking Cod. Takes all the standard baits — clams, squid, crab, worms.

FISHING SYSTEMS: Still Fishing; Drifting.

Pollock

Pollachius virens

DESCRIPTION: Although similar in shape and fin configuration to the Cod and Haddock, the Pollock is easily distinguished by its lack of markings, forked tail with pointed tips, and a pointed nose. Color usually is olive green to blue-green above, fading to gray or yellowish below.

SIZE: Averages 2-6 pounds, with fish up to 15 pounds or so not uncommon. May reach 40 pounds or slightly more. World record 50 pounds.

FOOD VALUE: Good. Coarser and less desirable than Cod or Haddock, but makes fine chowders and fish cakes.

GAME QUALITIES: By far the best sport fish of this family, Pollock strike artificial lures and wage a tough battle against light line.

TACKLE AND BAITS: When at or near the surface, usually in spring, Pollock are popular targets for all types of casting tackle—plug and spinning and even fly. They go for a variety of spoons, feathers, plugs and large streamer flies. However, they also are a mixed-bag target, along with Cod, Haddock and others, of partyboat and private boat anglers from Long Island to Newfoundland. Best baits are live or cut baitfish, but they also take the standard bottom-fishing baits.

FISHING SYSTEMS: Casting; Trolling; Still Fishing; Drifting.

OTHER NAMES:

Pollack
Boston Bluefish
Green Cod

RANGE: *Newfoundland to Chesapeake Bay. Not common south of Long Island.*

HABITAT: *Roams freely from the rocky shores out to the deep sea, and at any level from surface to bottom, depending on season and food availability. Many are caught from jetties and shoreline rocks, especially in Maine.*

Red Hake

Urophycis chuss

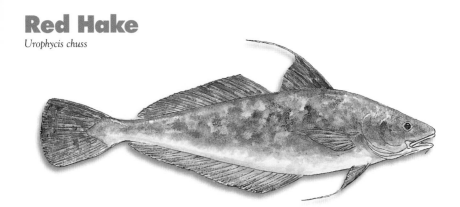

OTHER NAMES:

**Squirrel Hake
Squirrel Ling**

RANGE: North Carolina to Newfoundland.

HABITAT: Its wide range helps make it probably the most-caught Hake by sportsmen. Found from shore out to depths far beyond the reach of anglers.

DESCRIPTION: The back is olive; sides reddish and mottled; underparts white. The first dorsal fin sports a long streamer. Ventral fins also are streamer-like. The tail is slightly rounded. Inconspicuous chin barbel.

SIZE: Averages about 1-3 pounds; sometimes to 5 or 6 pounds. World record 7 pounds, 15 ounces.

FOOD VALUE: Excellent if fresh or properly iced and cared for, but the flesh is soft.

GAME QUALITIES: Fun to catch but no challenge.

TACKLE AND BAITS: Any tackle can be used, from spinning in shallow water to heavy bottom-fishing outfits in the deep. Most are included in potluck bags of bottom fish, and will hit clams, squid, shrimp, crab or cut fish.

FISHING SYSTEMS: Still Fishing; Drifting.

White Hake

Urophycis tenuis

DESCRIPTION: Very similar to the Red Hake but usually larger. The color is purple to brown above; yellowish below. Small black spots on belly. Small chin barbel.

SIZE: Most angling catches run 2-6 pounds, but maximum potential is about 50 pounds offshore. World record 46 pounds, 4 ounces.

FOOD VALUE: Excellent.

GAME QUALITIES: The biggest of the Hakes, it provides a brisk but short battle before being hauled from the depths.

TACKLE AND BAITS: Boat rods, medium reels, and lines to about 50-pound test are the norm—more to handle heavy terminal gear than the fish. Cut baitfish, squid and shrimp head a long list of good baits.

FISHING SYSTEMS: Still Fishing; Drifting.

OTHER NAMES:

**Mud Hake
Boston Ling**

RANGE: *North Carolina to Labrador*

HABITAT: *Mostly deep water, up to at least 500 feet. Many are caught by partyboats from the Mid-Atlantic states to Nova Scotia, although abundance varies a great deal.*

Silver Hake

Merluccius bilinearis

OTHER NAMES:

Whiting

RANGE: *South Carolina to Newfoundland.*

HABITAT: *Mostly deep water; small ones are taken near shore at times.*

DESCRIPTION: The back is dark gray or bluish; sides pale yellow; belly white to yellowish. Tail shallowly forked. No chin barbel.

SIZE: About 12 inches on average; a couple of pounds, tops. World record 4 pounds, 8 ounces.

FOOD VALUE: Excellent but soft-fleshed.

GAME QUALITIES: Not much tussle.

TACKLE AND BAITS: When fished in fairly shallow water, spinning tackle or very light saltwater tackle is best. As bait, live small baitfish and minnow-imitating lures, such as jigs and metallic squids are preferred, although it will also take squid and shrimp.

FISHING SYSTEMS: Still Fishing; Drifting; Casting.

Brosme brosme

DESCRIPTION: The Cusk is easily identified by long dorsal and anal fins of even height. At a glance, they appear to blend into the caudal, to give the appearance of one continuous fin that extends from just above the pectorals, around the tail, to the anal vent. Color is brown, with yellowish sides and dull white belly.

SIZE: Often runs 5-15 pounds; can reach at least 30 pounds. World record 35 pounds, 14 ounces.

FOOD VALUE: Very good.

GAME QUALITIES: Poor, but nearly always overpowered by heavy tackle.

TACKLE AND BAITS: Heavy bottom rigs and stout rods. Best baits are squid, clams and crabs.

FISHING SYSTEMS: Still Fishing; Drifting.

RANGE: Newfoundland to Cape Cod, straggling to New York.

HABITAT: Mostly very deep water, but is sometimes taken by bottom fishermen in as little as 50 feet.

Gameness and table quality make an ideal combination—a combination that accounts for the great appeal of the Snapper family in general, and the Red Snapper in particular, to partyboat anglers and other deepwater bottom fishermen in the South Atlantic states. They are seldom encountered inshore, however, except in Florida, where the Mangrove or Gray Snapper is a familiar inhabitant of bays and coastal streams of the entire state, and a few other types are shallow-water fixtures in South Florida and the Keys. Most species in the family are fitted with sharp and prominent canine teeth, which they are only too willing to sink into an unwary angler's hand. Whether their "snapping" is deliberate or simply a reflex action isn't really known but, regardless, it has given these fish their common family name.

The Snappers

Blackfin Snapper

Cubera Snapper

Dog Snapper

Gray Snapper

Lane Snapper

Mahogany Snapper

Mutton Snapper

Queen Snapper

Red Snapper

Schoolmaster

Silk Snapper

Vermilion Snapper

Yellowtail Snapper

Blackfin Snapper

Lutjanus buccanella

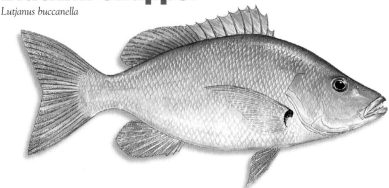

OTHER NAMES:

Blackspot Snapper
Bahamas Red Snapper

RANGE: *South Florida and Bermuda.*

HABITAT: *Blackfins are usually taken in depths of 200 feet or greater along sharp dropoffs.*

DESCRIPTION: The color is deep rose or brick red overall, with a black crescent-shaped mark at the base of the pectoral fin.

SIZE: Averages 3 or 4 pounds; usual maximum is 10 or so; possibly reaches 30 or more. World record 7 pounds, 3 ounces.

FOOD VALUE: Excellent.

GAME QUALITIES: A strong fighter—about like other Snappers its size.

TACKLE AND BAITS: Since they stay well beyond depths that permit anchoring by most pleasure boats, Blackfins are mostly taken by anglers drifting over outside deep cliffs and ledges. Heavy spinning and baitcasting tackle, or light-to-medium ocean gear is usually the tackle of choice. Blackfins eagerly strike a heavy bucktail or nylon jig, with or without a strip of fish or squid.

FISHING SYSTEMS: Drifting.

Cubera Snapper

Lutjanus cyanopterus

DESCRIPTION: In both shape and color, the Cubera looks much the same as a gigantic Gray Snapper. When comparing a small Cubera to a large Gray of roughly similar size, the only sure distinguishing feature is the patch of vomerine teeth on the inside roof of the mouth. In the Gray, this patch is shaped something like an arrow, with a shaft and a V-shaped head. That of the Cubera simply looks like a "V" without the shaft.

SIZE: The Cubera often reaches or exceeds 100 pounds, and the average is 30-50 pounds. It is definitely the giant of the Snapper family. World record 121 pounds, 8 ounces.

FOOD VALUE: Excellent to about 40 pounds. Larger ones tend to coarseness, and carry the possibility of causing Ciguatera poisoning (see Introduction).

GAME QUALITIES: A real brawler that uses its size, strength and every obstacle in the vicinity to great advantage.

TACKLE AND BAITS: Ocean gear with lines testing 50 pounds or more are generally needed, even though an occasional fish is caught on heavy spinning and plug tackle. Most Cuberas caught by design are taken at night off the Upper Keys during the summer months, fishing deep with whole live spiny lobsters for bait. Live blue crabs and live baitfish also work fairly well. Cuberas are perfectly willing to take dead baits too, but usually get beaten to them by smaller fish.

FISHING SYSTEMS: Drifting; Still Fishing.

OTHER NAMES:

Cuban Snapper
Cuban Dog
Snapper

RANGE: *Florida, rarely straggling farther north.*

HABITAT: *In Florida, most Cuberas are caught around wrecks and reef dropoffs in 100-200 feet of water, but they may surprise anglers at times in coastal creeks of South Florida and the Keys.*

Dog Snapper

Lutjanus jocu

OTHER NAMES:

Yellow Snapper
Jocu

RANGE: *South Florida to New England, but progressively more unusual north of Florida.*

HABITAT: *Adults mostly prowl the coral reefs of South Florida, while juveniles live in shallow rocky areas and along shorelines. Occasional catches elsewhere are usually made well offshore.*

DESCRIPTION: Color is light orange or yellow overall, darker on the back and lighter on the sides. The tail and dorsal fin are deep yellow or orange, while the other fins are lighter yellow. There is a broken blue streak below the eye and a white, V-shaped patch on the gill cover, under the blue markings. The name comes from the canine teeth, which seem even more prominent than in most other large Snappers.

SIZE: Most run only a couple of pounds, but the Dog Snapper is not uncommon at 10 or 15 pounds and can reach 30 or more. World record (Atlantic) 24 pounds.

FOOD VALUE: Excellent in all sizes.

GAME QUALITIES: A very strong and stubborn fighter.

TACKLE AND BAITS: Dog Snappers are less common than Gray Snappers but are taken on the same tackle and baits — usually light to medium ocean-fishing outfits with lines to 30-pound test. Best baits are live baitfish and cut ballyhoo or squid.

FISHING SYSTEMS: Still Fishing; Drifting.

Gray Snapper

Lutjanus griseus

DESCRIPTION: Generally from gray to dark green above, with a white underside. Usually has an overall reddish hue. A black line runs from the snout to the dorsal fin, transecting the eye. This line darkens when the fish is excited or actively feeding.

SIZE: Up to about 10 inches inshore, seldom larger. Grays average 2-6 pounds in deep water, and reach perhaps 20 pounds or more. Maximum size is undetermined due to confusion with the larger Cubera Snapper, which is very similar in coloration and body shape. World record 17 pounds.

FOOD VALUE: Excellent up to a pound or so. Large ones are stronger in taste but still very good.

GAME QUALITIES: Although small Grays are easy to catch on dead shrimp or cut fish and squid, larger always means wiser. Unless fishing at night, you're not apt to catch many good-size Grays unless you trim down the size of sinkers, hooks and leaders. When hooked, Gray Snappers make strong runs, then wage a bulldogging battle all the way to boatside.

TACKLE AND BAITS: For shallow fishing, spinning and light baitcasting rigs are best. Good baits include live shrimp, live minnows, fiddler crabs, cut shrimp, cut squid and cut baitfish. Many inshore snappers are also caught on lures and flies, especially along mangrove shorelines or around snags. Offshore, heavier spinning and baitcasting tackle, or light ocean tackle, are called for. Best to keep lines at 20-pound-test—or even 10 and 12, at times.

FISHING SYSTEMS: Still Fishing; Casting; Drifting.

OTHER NAMES:

Mangrove Snapper
Black Snapper
Mango
Caballerote

RANGE: South Florida to Cape Hatteras, straggling to Cape Cod; also Bermuda.

HABITAT: Juveniles are seasonally present in nearly all shallow waters and coastal estuaries of Florida, and are plentiful throughout the year in the southern half of Florida, the Caribbean and the Bahamas. Upon reaching a size of 10 or 12 inches, nearly all Gray Snapper switch their homes to deeper waters and are fished mostly over coral reefs, artificial reefs, wrecks and ledges, although big ones can also be caught in deep channels and passes along the coast.

Lane Snapper

Lutjanus synagris

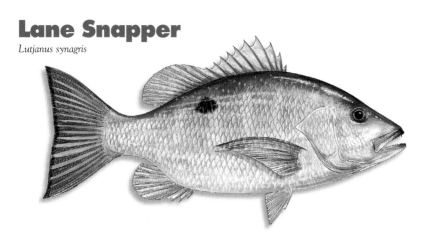

OTHER NAMES:

Spot Snapper
Candy Snapper
Biajaiba

RANGE: *South Florida to Cape Hatteras; also Bermuda.*

HABITAT: *Most are caught in fairly deep reef and offshore waters, but in the southern half of Florida, they also inhabit nearshore areas, and even bays. During times of warm water, they may come close to shore in the northern sectors as well. They seem to prefer broken or grassy bottom over rocky bottom.*

DESCRIPTION: Because it has a spot, the Lane is sometimes confused with a small Mutton Snapper. Both are rosy, but the lane has broken yellow bars along the sides, and its fins are mostly yellow. The single black spot on the side is larger, proportionately, than that of the Mutton. The anal fin is rounded.

SIZE: Most run well under 1 pound. Occasionally caught to 5 pounds in deep water. World record 7 pounds.

FOOD VALUE: Very good, but flesh is soft and must be kept well iced.

GAME QUALITIES: An aggressive striker of both natural and artificial baits, the Lane is fun to catch but is not a particularly strong fighter, even for its size.

TACKLE AND BAITS: Only very light tackle provides much sport. Productive baits include live and dead shrimp and also strips of cut squid or cut fish. Small jigs worked slowly near bottom are deadly.

FISHING SYSTEMS: Still Fishing; Casting; Drifting.

Mahogany Snapper

Lutjanus mahogoni

DESCRIPTION: The back and upper sides are tan to deep brown. The underside is silvery. There is a dark spot on the lateral line below the posterior dorsal fin, and the eye is large. The colors are vivid but with little of the red or pink that characterizes most tropical Snappers.

SIZE: To perhaps 3 pounds.

FOOD VALUE: Excellent.

GAME QUALITIES: As tough as any other small Snapper.

TACKLE AND BAITS: This is an odd catch that crops up now and then among mixed bags of small reef fish in South Florida. It will take small cutbaits and is a good match only for very light lines.

FISHING SYSTEMS: Still Fishing.

OTHER NAMES:

Ojonco

RANGE: Seldom seen north of South Florida, but straggles to Cape Hatteras.

HABITAT: Tropical reefs, although not common anywhere.

Mutton Snapper

Lutjanus analis

Mutton
Muttonfish

RANGE: Far more common in Florida (and Bermuda) than elsewhere, but occasionally taken off Georgia and the Carolinas and, rarely, as far north as Cape Cod.

HABITAT: In Florida and Bermuda, both adults and juveniles may be encountered on inshore grassbeds, coral patches and channels. Adults everywhere, however, mostly inhabit deeper reefs and banks.

DESCRIPTION: Adults are greenish above and red on the lower sides and underside. Juveniles are very bright, with an overall rosy appearance and mostly red fins. All sizes show blue lines on the gill covers and along the black, with a single black spot on the side just below the dorsal fin. Vague vertical bars may also be present. The anal fin is pointed.

SIZE: The average Mutton from deep water weighs at least 5 pounds, with individuals up to 15 pounds not uncommon. Maximum is probably around 35 pounds. World record 30 pounds, 4 ounces.

FOOD VALUE: Excellent.

GAME QUALITIES: Muttons are strong fighters in deep water, and can be dazzling in shallow water, getting off long runs and then resisting with strength and broad sides.

TACKLE AND BAITS: For deepwater angling, light to medium boat tackle is adequate, depending mostly on the depth being fished. Live small fish are always the very best of baits, but shrimp, squid and cutbaits are also productive, and deep-fished jigs take many fish. Light spinning or baitcasting tackle is an excellent choice inshore, when tossing jigs and plugs in channels or over grassbeds and rocks. Sighted Mutton Snapper can also be induced to take a large streamer fly.

FISHING SYSTEMS: Still Fishing; Casting; Drifting.

Queen Snapper

Etelis oculatus

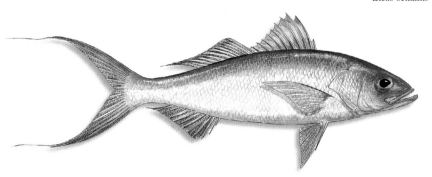

DESCRIPTION: Color is bright red and the shape is slender. The most handsome feature is its deeply forked red tail that continues to lengthen as the fish grows larger. The eye is very large and yellow.

SIZE: Usually runs 3 to 5 pounds; occasionally to 20 pounds or so. World record 11 pounds, 11 ounces.

FOOD VALUE: Excellent.

GAME QUALITIES: Not much, because of the tackle required.

TACKLE AND BAITS: Cutbaits fished very deep with heavy weights and motorized gear.

FISHING SYSTEMS: Drifting.

RANGE: *Florida and Bermuda.*

HABITAT: *Another deepwater type, it is most common at depths of 500 feet or more, but it does sometimes turn up as a curiosity on the lines of Grouper fishermen working in 200 or 250 feet of water.*

Red Snapper

Lutjanus campechanus

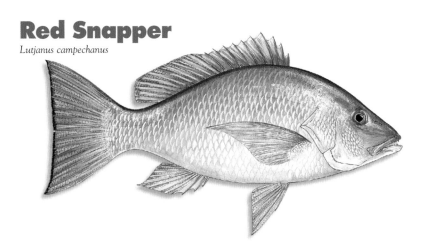

OTHER NAMES:

**North American Red Snapper
Genuine Red Snapper
Pargo Colorado**

RANGE: Central Florida to Cape Hatteras, straggling southward to South Florida, and northward to New Jersey.

HABITAT: Juveniles are occasionally encountered near shore, but the great majority of Red Snapper fall to bottom fishermen over deep offshore banks in 100 to 200 feet of water.

DESCRIPTION: Bright rosy red is the usual color, the red deepening as the fish grows larger. The canine teeth are present but less prominent than those of the Gray or Mutton Snapper. The eye is red and the anal fin triangular.

SIZE: Common from a couple of pounds to 10 pounds, but reaches 20 pounds or more with some frequency. Maximum potential is about 50 pounds. World record 50 pounds, 4 ounces.

FOOD VALUE: Excellent at all sizes.

GAME QUALITIES: A hard-fighting fish that uses strong, head-shaking tactics rather than long runs.

TACKLE AND BAITS: Few Red Snapper spots are shallow enough to permit the use of light tackle. Generally, the fishing takes place on headboats or long-range charterboats and requires deep drops, often in strong current. This means that only very heavy rods and strong lines of 50- or 80-pound test can handle the heavy weights needed to do the job. As for baits, dead Cigar Minnows, Pilchards or cut fish and squid do well at times, although in heavily fished spots it might be necessary to use live small baitfish to coax bites from Snappers of decent size.

FISHING SYSTEMS: Still Fishing; Drifting.

Schoolmaster

Lutjanus apodus

DESCRIPTION: This colorful Snapper is deep-bodied and yellowish, with vertical white bars. In large specimens, however, the stripes may be nearly invisible. The Schoolmaster, however, does not have a white, cone-shaped patch on the gill.

SIZE: Averages a pound or less in shallow water. Big individuals on the deep reefs may reach 6 or 7 pounds. World record 13 pounds, 4 ounces.

FOOD VALUE: Excellent.

GAME QUALITIES: A tough foe, like other Snappers.

TACKLE AND BAITS: Since most catches are small, spinning and baitcasting outfits easily do the job. Shrimp, squid and small fish are all acceptable baits.

FISHING SYSTEMS: Still Fishing; Drifting.

OTHER NAMES:

Barred Snapper

RANGE: *South Florida, rarely straggling farther north.*

HABITAT: *Juveniles are plentiful in shallow coastal waters. As they grow, they work into deeper water, where dense schools are often encountered by divers.*

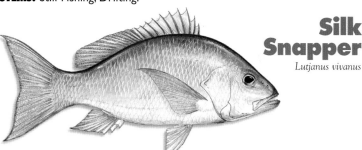

Silk Snapper

Lutjanus vivanus

DESCRIPTION: Pink overall and shaped like more familiar Snappers, the Silk can be identified by its yellow eye.

SIZE: Average 3 to 5 pounds. The maximum is uncertain, but fish larger than 15 pounds are occasionally taken. World record 18 pounds, 5 ounces.

FOOD VALUE: Many rate it best of the Snappers.

GAME QUALITIES: Little battle, thanks to great depth and electric reels usually used.

TACKLE AND BAITS: With rare exception, they are taken by stout rods, using cutbait weighted by several pounds of lead.

FISHING SYSTEMS: Specialized deep systems only.

OTHER NAMES:

Yelloweye Snapper

RANGE: *South Florida to Cape Hatteras.*

HABITAT: *Usually beyond the range of sporting tackle—in at least 300 feet of water but more commonly at 100 fathoms and deeper.*

Vermilion Snapper

Rhomboplites aurorubens

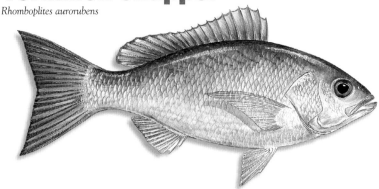

OTHER NAMES:

Beeliner
Mingo
Cajon

RANGE: Central Florida to Cape Hatteras; also Bermuda.

HABITAT: Prefers the same depths as the Red Snapper, with which it often mixes. A common panfish offshore.

DESCRIPTION: Similar to the Red Snapper in color but easily distinguished from it—in addition to smaller size—by the lack of canine teeth, and by its rounded anal fin. Color is rosy red on back and sides, fading to pinkish and then whitish below. The fins are red and the eye very large.

SIZE: Averages less than a pound; rarely to 5 pounds or slightly larger. World record 7 pounds, 3 ounces.

FOOD VALUE: An excellent panfish.

GAME QUALITIES: Poor. Most are caught on heavy tackle at considerable depth while fishing for Red Snapper or other larger game.

TACKLE AND BAITS: When conditions are favorable enough to permit getting down with weights of an ounce or so, spinning and baitcasting tackle are more productive fun, but this is seldom possible, so most are yanked up with little fight on big tackle. Beeliners usually bite greedily at any sort of small dead bait, including cut fish, squid and shrimp.

FISHING SYSTEMS: Still Fishing; Drifting.

Yellowtail Snapper

Ocyurus chrysurus

DESCRIPTION: Yellowtails don't have the family looks, even though they definitely are Snappers. The body is long and streamlined. A yellow stripe runs the full length of the body from forward of the eye to the deeply forked yellow tail. The stripe is very vivid in young fish, but pales as the fish grows.

SIZE: From less than a foot in coastal shallows to an average of 1-3 pounds over outside patches and ledges. "Flags" running 5 pounds are common around deepwater dropoffs. World record 8 pounds, 9 ounces.

FOOD VALUE: Excellent if fresh or well iced.

GAME QUALITIES: Ranks among the best fighters of the coral reefs. Because most are hooked high in the water column, they usually make long, strong runs against light tackle.

TACKLE AND BAIT: Undersize fish in the shallows will greedily hit nearly any bait or lure. Yellowtails of decent size, however, are among the wariest of biters, generally requiring lighter lines, leaders, hooks and sinkers than the angler would really like to use. At least this adds greatly to the thrill and suspense of the battle. Regulars mostly try to get by with spinning tackle and 15-pound line, but on many days must go to 12-pound lines or smaller, to produce or sustain any action. Small dead baits—cut fish, cut squid and pieces of shrimp—catch the most Yellowtails because those baits are similar in size and buoyancy to the ground chum that is used to lure them close.

FISHING SYSTEMS: Still Fishing; Drifting; Trolling; Casting.

OTHER NAMES:

Tail
Flag
Rabirubia

RANGE: *Common only in South Florida and Bermuda, although occasionally caught along the coast as far north as Massachusetts.*

HABITAT: *Small fish grow up around shallow coastal reefs and patches. Best fishing depth in most areas is from 60 to about 120 feet, with nearly all the "Flags" coming from the deepest habitat.*

Because Groupers are basically warm-water fishes, Florida (and Bermuda) are home to the greatest quantity and variety of these popular bottom dwellers. A few types, however, are widely distributed along the Atlantic coast, and are caught even as far north as New England on rare occasion. In Georgia and the Carolinas, as well as in Florida, Groupers are among the mainstays of offshore bottom fishermen, just as Cods and their relatives are in icier waters. The range of sizes is also broad, with a couple of species—such as the Jewfish—reaching several hundred pounds, while others scale no more than a few ounces. In Florida, some types of Groupers are also fishable in shallow water by trollers and casters—even fly fishermen. The Black Sea Bass, familiar to anglers almost everywhere on the Atlantic Coast, is a member of this same family, as is the even smaller Sand Perch.

The Groupers

Black Grouper

Black Sea Bass

Coney

Gag

Graysby

Jewfish

Marbled Grouper

Misty Grouper

Nassau Grouper

Red Grouper

Red Hind

Sand Perch

Scamp

Snowy Grouper

Speckled Hind

Tiger Grouper

Warsaw Grouper

Yellowedge Grouper

Yellowfin Grouper

Yellowmouth Grouper

Black Grouper

Mycteroperca bonaci

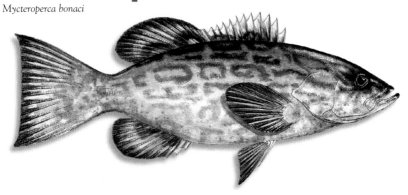

OTHER NAMES:

**Bonaci Arara
Aguaji**

RANGE: Mainly South Florida and Bermuda, but is taken less frequently along the Atlantic Coast to Cape Cod.

HABITAT: Various age groups inhabit coral reef areas in South Florida. Most of the big fish everywhere, however, prefer offshore reefs, banks and wrecks, in from about 30 feet of water out to at least 300 feet.

DESCRIPTION: The color is similar to that of the Gag, but the markings are darker and they usually form box-like shapes. Fins are black, with either black or deep blue edges.

SIZE: A large Grouper, the Black frequently exceeds 50 pounds in weight and is not rare at 100 pounds or slightly more. World record 114 pounds.

FOOD VALUE: Excellent.

GAME QUALITIES: Considered best of the Groupers.

TACKLE AND BAITS: In deep water, heavy outfits with line of at least 50-pound-test is advisable, although much lighter tackle in experienced hands has taken many very big Blacks in Florida. For drifting or still fishing, the best baits are frisky live fish, such as Blue Runners or other small jacks. Pinfish and Pilchards are good too, as are Mullet heads and other large cut-baits. Best casting lures are leadhead jigs, weighing from 1-4 ounces, depending on depth. Trolling over the reefs with rigged, swimming Mullet, feather-and-strip combos, and large plugs also takes many.

FISHING SYSTEMS: Drifting; Still Fishing; Trolling; Casting.

Black Sea Bass

Centropristis striata

DESCRIPTION: Adult color is black with blue highlights and tiny white spots or stripes on the dorsal fin. An indistinct pattern sometimes is present on the sides, especially in small fish. Large males have a hump on the back forward of the dorsal, and the dorsal, anal and caudal fins have feathery edges.

SIZE: Although Sea Bass of 8 pounds or more are in the records, individuals weighing more than a couple of pound are increasingly uncommon. World record 9 pounds, 8 ounces.

FOOD VALUE: Excellent. White, mild flesh.

GAME QUALITIES: A hard and willing striker, and strong for its usually modest size.

TACKLE AND BAITS: Light spinning and baitcasting tackle are the best choices. Will take live or dead shrimp, squid, seaworms and all sorts of cutbaits, along with live small baitfish and artificial jigs and underwater plugs.

FISHING SYSTEMS: Still Fishing; Casting; Trolling; Drifting.

OTHER NAMES:

Sea Bass
Black Bass
Blackfish
Rockfish

RANGE: Central Florida to Cape Cod, straggling to Nova Scotia.

HABITAT: Widely at home, both offshore and inshore. Likes rocky areas, wrecks, channels with hard bottom, jetties, and deep holes in grass flats. Larger fish mostly stay well offshore.

Coney

Epinephelus fulvus

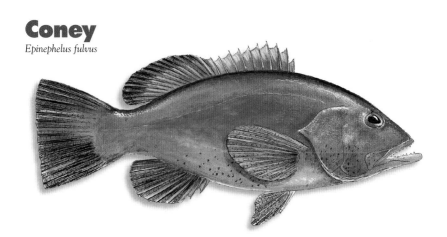

OTHER NAMES:

**Golden Coney
Golden Grouper
Guativere**

RANGE: South Florida and Bermuda.

HABITAT: Coral reefs and inshore coral patches.

DESCRIPTION: This fellow is common in several color phases, and these variations fool many anglers into believing that each is a separate species. The most frequent phases include vivid yellow or gold; bicolor gold-and-brown; bicolor red-and-brown.

SIZE: Most run 6-8 inches; maximum is no more than a foot.

FOOD VALUE: Not much to work with.

GAME QUALITIES: Strikes aggressively, sometimes on surprisingly large lures, but is too small to put up any fight.

TACKLE AND BAITS: Never targeted. If it were, only ultralight spinning tackle would be chosen. Takes a variety of both baits and lures fished for larger species.

FISHING SYSTEMS: Still Fishing; Casting.

Gag

Mycteroperca microlepis

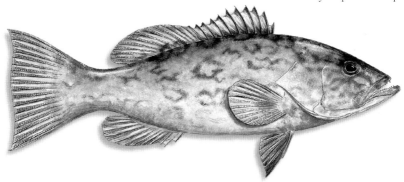

DESCRIPTION: When first pulled from the water, the color is bright and bold—gray or light brown with wavy markings on the side and fins that are edged in blue. After death, the color deepens and becomes an overall dark brown.

SIZE: Can top 50 pounds in deep water, and has been recorded to 80 pounds, but 20-30 is the usual maximum range. Small juveniles weighing from less than a pound to 3 or 4 pounds are often caught inshore. World record 80 pounds, 6 ounces.

FOOD VALUE: Excellent. The flesh is firm and white with only small streaks of red.

GAME QUALITIES: Strikes aggressively and is a tough foe at all depths.

TACKLE AND BAITS: Offshore bottom fishermen tend toward stout rods with 50- and 80-pound-test lines. Some anglers catch Gags routinely on spinning and plug tackle. This is also the best of the Groupers for fly fishermen, since they are frequently found in fairly shallow water and will eagerly take a large streamer fly. Hard-lure casters use leadhead jigs, mostly, while trollers rely on large deep-diving plugs. Live baitfish of various sorts are the best natural offerings—try Pilchards, Menhaden or Pinfish. Dead small fish and large cutbaits also work well.

FISHING SYSTEMS: Still Fishing; Drifting; Trolling; Casting.

OTHER NAMES:

Gray Grouper
Black Grouper
Grass Grouper
Copper Belly

RANGE: Florida to Cape Hatteras, straggling to Cape Cod; also Bermuda.

HABITAT: In some areas of Florida, both juveniles and adults frequent inshore holes and ledges, often on deeper grass flats. From there they can be found around structure at virtually any fishable offshore depth.

Graysby

Epinephelus cruentatus

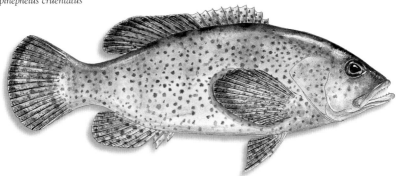

OTHER NAMES:

Enjambre
Cuna Cabrilla

RANGE: South Florida and Bermuda.

HABITAT: Coral reefs and patches.

DESCRIPTION: The color is usually gray with many tiny red or brown dots all over the sides and fins. Four dark blotches are in a line just under the dorsal fin.

SIZE: Under 1 foot. World record 2 pounds, 8 ounces.

FOOD VALUE: Not much.

GAME QUALITIES: Like the Coney, it is belligerent but without the muscle or size to match.

TACKLE AND BAITS: This is a common reef catch when small cutbaits are used in hopes of bagging Yellowtail, Grunts or Porgies.

FISHING SYSTEMS: Still Fishing.

Jewfish

Epinephelus itajara

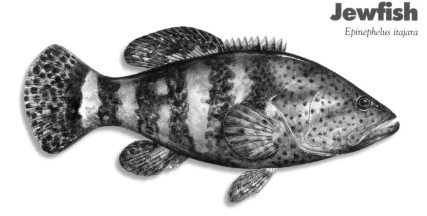

DESCRIPTION: At any size, there's no mistaking a Jewfish. Juveniles are brilliantly marked with irregular dark brown blotches against a light brown or gray background, extending from head to tail. Numerous black spots are usually present as well on head, sides and fins. Adults are easily identified by size alone, but they have the same patterns in more subdued shades of brown that are not so brilliantly contrasted. The tail is round, as are the posterior dorsal, anal and pectoral fins.

SIZE: Historically, anywhere from 5 to 200 pounds on average, and topping 500 pounds on occasion. World record 680 pounds.

FOOD VALUE: Small ones excellent and big ones darn good—which was the main reason for their precipitous decline and total closure in the 1980s.

GAME QUALITIES: Giant Jewfish around deep wrecks defy the heaviest sporting tackle. Inshore juveniles are great battlers on casting gear.

TACKLE AND BAITS: Baitcasting, spinning and even fly tackle make acceptable matchups for the inshore fish, which will—and often do—hit the full range of lures and flies that are used by casters seeking Snook and Tarpon. Again, though, it takes all the muscle you and your tackle can come up with to battle Jewfish of 100 pounds or more. Best natural baits are live Jack or Catfish inshore; live or dead large fish for offshore giants—including Bonito and Amberjack up to 15 pounds or more.

FISHING SYSTEMS: Still Fishing; Drift Fishing; Casting.

OTHER NAMES:

Spotted Jewfish
Great Grouper
Guasa Mero

RANGE: Florida and Bermuda, straggling to South Carolina.

HABITAT: Juveniles frequent mangrove-lined canals, creeks and bays. Adults can be found at a variety of depths, from holes and channels of coastal waters out to offshore ledges and reefs; also around pilings of bridges and under deepwater docks and piers.

Marbled Grouper

Epinephelus inermis

RANGE: *South Florida and Bermuda.*

HABITAT: *Very deep dropoffs or seamounts in 500 feet or more of water.*

DESCRIPTION: Deeper-bodied than most Groupers, its shape is reminiscent of the unrelated Tripletail. Color is dark brown or charcoal with numerous white spots.

SIZE: Averages 5-10 pounds; sometimes exceeds 20. World record 10 pounds, 8 ounces.

FOOD VALUE: Excellent, as are all the Groupers that inhabit very deep water.

GAME QUALITIES: Seldom caught on sporting gear.

TACKLE AND BAITS: Power reels and cut baitfish or squid.

FISHING SYSTEMS: Drifting.

Misty Grouper

Epinephelus mystacinus

OTHER NAMES:

Mystic Grouper
Mustache Grouper

RANGE: *South Florida and Bermuda.*

HABITAT: *Rocks and ledges at 500 feet or more.*

DESCRIPTION: Color is brown with 6 to 9 vertical whitish bars.

SIZE: Common at 15-50 pounds; exceeds 100 pounds.

FOOD VALUE: Excellent.

GAME QUALITIES: Not taken with manual tackle.

TACKLE AND BAITS: Power reels with cutbait.

FISHING SYSTEMS: Drifting.

Nassau Grouper

Epinephelus striatus

DESCRIPTION: At a glance, it looks very much like a Red Grouper in shape and pattern, although the basic coloration tends more to brown or gray than reddish. The sure distinguishing feature is a black blotch on the caudal peduncle, forward of the tail fin.

SIZE: Common at 1-10 pounds. May reach 30 or more. World record 38 pounds, 8 ounces.

FOOD VALUE: Excellent, but possession prohibited in U.S. waters.

GAME QUALITIES: Very tough—just like the Red Grouper.

TACKLE AND BAITS: Most are caught by potluck reef or creek fishermen on light ocean gear or stout bait-casting and spinning outfits—all using lines of 12-20 pounds. Cut fish, conch or squid all make good baits, and they will also strike jigs, spoons and underwater or surface plugs. Bigger fish on rough coral reefs require heavy tackle for bottom-fishing, and can also be caught by trolling with feather-and-strip baits or with large swimming plugs.

FISHING SYSTEMS: Still Fishing; Trolling; Drifting.

OTHER NAMES:

White Grouper
Rockfish
Bahamas
 Grouper
Cherna Criolla

RANGE: *South Florida to Cape Hatteras; also Bermuda.*

HABITAT: *Prefers coral reefs, and probably does not roam into water much deeper than 120 feet or so. In South Florida and Bermuda, small specimens may be found over inshore patches, and also in creeks and channels.*

Red Grouper

Epinephelus morio

RANGE: *South Florida to Cape Hatteras, straggling to Cape Cod; also Bermuda.*

HABITAT: *Widely distributed, from close inshore (in some areas of Florida) to ledges and wrecks in up to 300 or so feet. Most sporting catches are made in water up to 200 feet deep.*

DESCRIPTION: Overall coloration is light red or rusty red with whitish spots and large, dark blotches. No black mark forward of the tail fin.

SIZE: Common at 1-10 pounds; maximum perhaps 40 pounds. World record 42 pounds, 4 ounces.

FOOD VALUE: Good.

GAME QUALITIES: The Red is possibly the toughest-fighting Grouper, pound-for-pound. Although they will "hole up" like other Groupers, many are hooked on light and fairly light tackle in areas where cover is well scattered, and this gives them the chance to demonstrate their gameness to best advantage.

TACKLE AND BAITS: Stout spinning and baitcasting tackle, with 15- or 20-pound line, can do the job in water less than 100 feet deep. Offshore, the standard tackle is a boat outfit with 40-pound line or more. Reds will hit all the baits and lures recommended for Gag and other Groupers, but they are also very fond of crustacean baits, particularly shrimp and crab. They are ready strikers on leadhead jigs, fished with light tackle.

FISHING SYSTEMS: Still Fishing; Drifting; Trolling.

Red Hind

Epinephelus guttatus

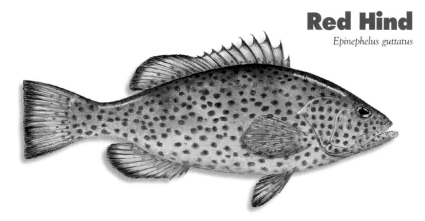

DESCRIPTION: Has a measled appearance, with numerous bright red spots on a tan or creamy red background. The caudal, anal and posterior dorsal fins are edged in black.

SIZE: Usual catch is 1 or 2 pounds; rarely reaches 5 pounds. World record 6 pounds, 1 ounce.

FOOD VALUE: Excellent.

GAME QUALITIES: Aggressive striker but a lethargic battler.

TACKLE AND BAITS: In rather shallow reef areas, Red Hinds can be caught by drifting and bouncing the bottom with leadhead jigs weighing up to one ounce. Spinning or baitcasting tackle is used for this work. Farther offshore, most are caught on heavy gear aimed at bigger Groupers. Any sort of cutbait looks good to the Red Hind.

FISHING SYSTEMS: Drifting; Still Fishing; Casting.

OTHER NAMES:

Strawberry Grouper
Sandwich Grouper
Cabrilla
Tofia

RANGE: *Florida, straggling to Cape Hatteras; also Bermuda.*

HABITAT: *Coral reefs.*

Rock Hind

Epinephelus adscensionis

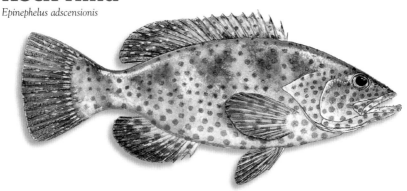

OTHER NAMES:

Rock Cod
Cabre Mora
Mero Cabrilla

RANGE: Same as the Red Hind.

HABITAT: Coral reefs and rocky banks.

DESCRIPTION: Appearance is very similar to the Red Hind, but this close relative is mostly brown or tan in background color. It does have the same small red spots, but also has large, dark blotches on the upper sides — usually two, but often more.

SIZE: About the same as the Red Hind, but maximum may be slightly larger — to perhaps 8 or 9 pounds. World record 9 pounds.

FOOD VALUE: Excellent.

GAME QUALITIES: Like the Red Hind, an eager striker but a poor battler.

TACKLE AND BAITS: Same as for the Red Hind.

FISHING SYSTEMS: Drifting; Still Fishing.

Sand Perch

Diplectrum formosum

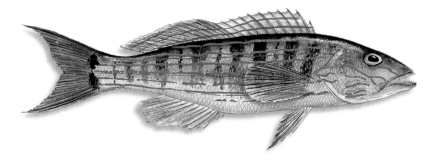

DESCRIPTION: The shape is slender and cylindrical. The mouth is large and the tail wide. Color is tan with brown vertical bars or blotches, and full-length horizontal lines of blue and orange.

SIZE: Averages 6-8 inches; rarely larger.

FOOD VALUE: A tasty panfish and very meaty for its size.

GAME QUALITIES: A willing striker and battler, but too small to put up real resistance.

TACKLE AND BAITS: Sand Perch are often fished for deliberately, either for supper or for bait. Best tackle is a light spinning outfit. Small jigs, either plain or tipped with a piece of shrimp or cutbait, will produce the most, but any sort of bottom rig and natural bait will do the job.

FISHING SYSTEMS: Still Fishing; Drifting.

OTHER NAMES:

Squirrelfish

RANGE: Florida to Cape Hatteras.

HABITAT: Found from bays and shorelines to well offshore over a variety of bottoms. Seems to prefer rather open bottom with patches of grass or scattered rock.

Scamp

Mycteroperca phenax

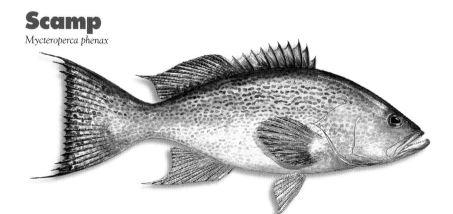

OTHER NAMES:

Brown Grouper
Broomtail
 Grouper
Abadejo

RANGE: Florida to Cape Hatteras, straggling north to Cape Cod.

HABITAT: Generally found well offshore, over deep banks, ledges or dropoffs in 100 feet of water or more.

DESCRIPTION: Elongated rays of the caudal fin give the broomtail appearance reflected in one of its common names. Color is a deep tan or chocolate brown, with numerous darker markings that form dots, or lines, or groups of lines.

SIZE: Usually under 10 pounds, but can top 20. World record 29 pounds.

FOOD VALUE: Excellent. Ranks commercially as the most desirable Grouper.

GAME QUALITIES: Fights long and strong on light tackle, but most are overpowered by heavy gear.

TACKLE AND BAITS: Sheer depth—typical of many headboat excursions—necessitates rods and lines stout enough to handle very heavy sinkers. Any kind of small fish makes a fine live bait. Shrimp, squid and cutbaits also do the job.

FISHING SYSTEMS: Still Fishing; Drifting; Trolling.

Snowy Grouper

Epinephelus niveatus

DESCRIPTION: Dark gray or brown in color, liberally sprinkled with white spots.

SIZE: The average is 5-10 pounds; said to reach 50 pounds. World record 23 pounds.

FOOD VALUE: Excellent.

GAME QUALITIES: Not caught on sporting tackle.

TACKLE AND BAITS: Power reels; cutbaits.

FISHING SYSTEMS: Drifting.

OTHER NAMES:

Golden Grouper

RANGE: Florida to Cape Hatteras, straggling to Cape Cod.

HABITAT: Small ones may come in as shallow as 250-300 feet on occasion, but most stick to 600-1,000 feet.

Speckled Hind

Epinephelus drummondhayi

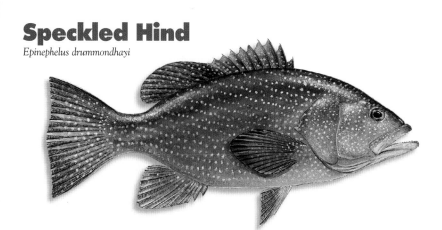

OTHER NAMES:

Kitty Mitchell
Calico Grouper

RANGE: *South Florida to Cape Hatteras; also Bermuda.*

HABITAT: *Once in a while, bottom-fishermen will catch one in around 200 feet of water, but their usual habitat is in much deeper water—300 to 600 feet—around ledges or outcroppings.*

DESCRIPTION: Color is most often a dark gray or brown, with many small, yellowish or white spots on sides, gill covers and fins, but some are light tan or yellow with whiter spots.

SIZE: Most catches range from 5 to 20 pounds; maximum is around 40 pounds. World record 52 pounds, 8 ounces.

FOOD VALUE: This and the other deepwater Groupers are considered even better table fare than their relatives in shallow water.

GAME QUALITIES: Seldom caught on sporting gear.

TACKLE AND BAITS: Electric reels and wire line. Any kind of cutbait seems to work well.

FISHING SYSTEMS: Drifting.

Tiger Grouper

Mycteroperca tigris

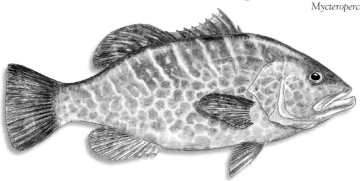

DESCRIPTION: Vivid oblique stripes on the upper sides provide the "Tiger" stripes. Smaller wormlike markings are situated on the lower sides and fins.

SIZE: A medium-size Grouper, averaging under 10 pounds and probably not reaching 20. World record 14 pounds, 8 ounces.

FOOD VALUE: Excellent.

GAME QUALITIES: Very tough on a pound-for-pound basis.

TACKLE: Not specifically targeted—as Blacks or Gags often are—most tigers are caught by anglers potluck fishing over the reefs. Best baits are small live fish and fresh cut fish or squid. Like others of their clan, Tigers will take a variety of artificials, including jigs and trolling plugs.

FISHING SYSTEMS: Still Fishing; Drifting; Trolling; Casting.

OTHER NAMES:

Bonaci Gato

RANGE: *South Florida and Bermuda.*

HABITAT: *Coral reefs.*

Warsaw Grouper

Epinephelus nigritus

OTHER NAMES:

Giant Grouper
Black Jewfish
Garrupa Negrita

RANGE: *Florida to Cape Cod.*

HABITAT: *Very deep dropoffs, ledges and seamounts. Seldom encountered in less than 200 feet, and most common in much deeper water.*

DESCRIPTION: The only other Grouper that could be confused (at similar sizes) with the Jewfish, it is easily distinguished by the tail, which is square instead of round, and by an elongated, crestlike dorsal spine. Color is mottled dark brown, shading to slightly lighter brown on lower portions.

SIZE: Commonly caught at 30-80 pounds, with 100-pounders not rare. Grows to more than 500. World record 436 pounds, 12 ounces.

FOOD VALUE: Good.

GAME QUALITIES: A tough customer. Has great strength to go with great bulk.

TACKLE AND BAITS: Only the heaviest rods, large reels and lines testing 80 pounds or more are really adequate. Catches on lighter tackle are possible but opportunistic and rare, and usually of smaller specimens. Fairly large whole fish, or halved Bonito and other hefty cutbaits are all productive.

FISHING SYSTEMS: Still Fishing; Drifting.

Yellowedge Grouper

Epinephelus flavolimbatus

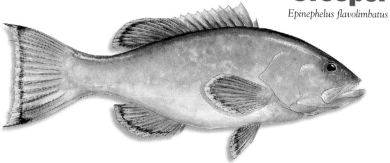

DESCRIPTION: Color is light brown with darker mottling. The dorsal, pectoral and anal fins all have yellow outer edges, underlined with black.

SIZE: Averages 5 or 10 pounds; may exceed 30 pounds. World record 41 pounds, 1 ounce.

FOOD VALUE: Excellent.

GAME QUALITIES: A good fighter, but not often hooked with sporting tackle.

TACKLE AND BAITS: Power reels are best, with heavy manual rods and reels possible in rare instances. Cut fish or squid make the best bait.

FISHING SYSTEMS: Drifting.

OTHER NAMES:

Deepwater Yellowfin Grouper

RANGE: Florida.

HABITAT: Over deep coral reefs at times, but prefers 300 feet and more.

Yellowfin Grouper

Mycteroperca venenosa

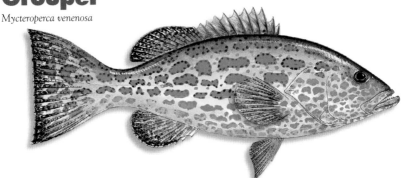

OTHER NAMES:

Strawberry Grouper

RANGE: *Florida and Bermuda.*

HABITAT: *About the same as that of the Black Grouper.*

DESCRIPTION: Color varies. Most specimens are decked out in one of two color phases—black or strawberry. In its strawberry phase, the Yellowfin is the prettiest of all the Groupers—overall bright red with dark red or brown box-shaped blotches. The black phase would make it almost a dead ringer for the Black Grouper except for the bright yellow trim on the pectoral and dorsal fins. The yellow trim remains, regardless of the other color variations.

SIZE: This is a hefty Grouper, often running to 15 pounds or so, and sometimes to 30. The smaller ones, from 3-10 pounds, are usually the most brightly colored. World record 40 pounds, 12 ounces.

FOOD VALUE: Smaller fish are excellent.

GAME QUALITIES: An outstanding fighter.

TACKLE AND BAITS: Even though Yellowfins average smaller than Blacks, it is still a good idea to stick with heavy tackle in deep water, reserving light gear, such as heavy spinning and baitcasting outfits, for the shallow inshore patches. Live fish make the very best baits, although cutbaits work pretty well most of the time. Best casting lures are leadhead jigs. Trolling over the reefs with rigged, swimming Mullet, feather-and-strip combinations, or large diving plugs is effective too.

FISHING SYSTEMS: Still Fishing; Drifting; Trolling; Casting.

Yellowmouth Grouper

Mycteroperca interstitialis

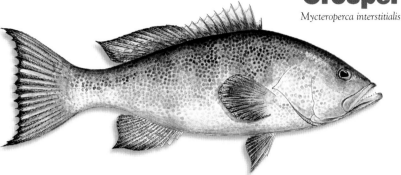

DESCRIPTION: Virtually identical in appearance to the Scamp, but distinguishable by the inside of the mouth, which is yellow.

SIZE: Averages 2-3 pounds; maximum probably less than 10 pounds. World record 13 pounds.

FOOD VALUE: Excellent.

GAME QUALITIES: A tough fighter on tackle of reasonable size.

TACKLE AND BAITS: Seldom targeted, but responds about the same as the Scamp, although it is much less plentiful in waters of sportfishing depth.

FISHING SYSTEMS: Still Fishing; Trolling; Drifting.

OTHER NAMES:

Salmon Rockfish

RANGE: *South Florida and Bermuda.*

HABITAT: *Not often encountered in the shallows, it sticks to water of 100-200 feet—or even deeper—usually in the vicinity of dropoffs.*

Although not considered great sport fish, Grunts are fun to catch and make fine table fare. Many southern anglers, in fact, class a mess of "grits and grunts" as among the best of all fish dishes. Grunts, moreover, are usually willing to bite, even when more desirable bottom species play hard to get. Theirs is a large family which lists most of its member as residents of the tropics or subtropics, but a few of them wander widely through temperate waters of the Atlantic Coast. The species included in this chapter are representative of the group, and also the ones that are large enough to be of any real interest to sportsmen.

The Grunts

Black Margate

Bluestriped Grunt

French Grunt

Margate

Pigfish

Porkfish

Tomtate

White Grunt

Black Margate

Anisotremus surinamensis

OTHER NAMES:

Black Bream
Surf Bream
Pompon

RANGE: *Florida, straggling to South Carolina.*

HABITAT: *Many are caught from the surf near groins or jetties, or around rocks, but it roams widely from the shore to fairly deep offshore water.*

DESCRIPTION: The body is deep, the dorsal spines heavy and the lips thick—all of which makes the Black Margate appear more closely related to the Croakers.

SIZE: Often taken at 3-4 pounds and may top 10. World record 12 pounds, 12 ounces.

FOOD VALUE: Good.

GAME QUALITIES: Strong fighter on light gear.

TACKLE AND BAITS: Spinning, baitcasting and surf tackle, along with the light classes of ocean tackle. Shrimp, clams and sand fleas are probably the best.

FISHING SYSTEMS: Still Fishing; Drifting.

Bluestriped Grunt

Haemulon sciurus

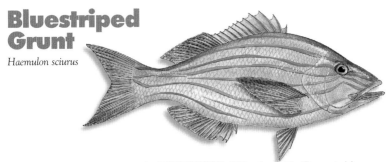

OTHER NAMES:

Blue Grunt
Yellow Grunt
Ronco Amarillo

RANGE: *South Florida to Cape Hatteras, but rare north of Florida; also Bermuda.*

HABITAT: *Coral reefs; also inshore coral patches and channels.*

DESCRIPTION: Whether this Grunt is blue or yellow is in the eye of the beholder. It's body is yellow, but the vivid blue stripes may dominate the angler's eye.

SIZE: Averages 8-10 inches; sometimes exceeds 12.

FOOD VALUE: Very good.

GAME QUALITIES: A strong fighter on light gear.

TACKLE AND BAITS: Light spinning and baitcasting outfits. Live or dead shrimp and cut fish are the standard baits. Cut squid is also productive, and small lures pay off on occasion.

FISHING SYSTEMS: Still Fishing; Drifting.

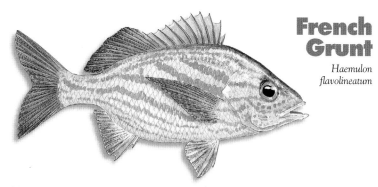

French Grunt

Haemulon flavolineatum

DESCRIPTION: Another very colorful type, this one is dingy white overall with many bright yellow lines on the sides, yellow fins and a red mouth.

SIZE: Averages 6-8 inches; rarely to one foot.

FOOD VALUE: Very good.

GAME QUALITIES: Fun on very light gear.

TACKLE AND BAITS: Light spinning and baitcasting tackle, with cut shrimp or cut fish as bait.

FISHING SYSTEMS: Still Fishing; Drifting.

OTHER NAMES:

**Yellow Grunt
Corocoro
Ronco Contenado**

RANGE: *South Florida to Cape Hatteras, but rare north of Florida; also Bermuda.*

HABITAT: *Coral reefs; inshore patches and channels.*

Margate

Haemulon album

DESCRIPTION: Very much like the white grunt, but the sides are very white and pearly, and the fins are darker.

SIZE: This is the largest of the Grunts, frequently 4 pounds. Record 15 pounds, 12 ounces.

FOOD VALUE: Good.

GAME QUALITIES: Fights like a Snapper.

TACKLE AND BAITS: Difficult to target, most are caught on cutbaits by bottom fishermen.

FISHING SYSTEMS: Still Fishing; Drifting.

OTHER NAMES:

**White Margate
Margate Grunt
Ronco Blanco**

RANGE: *Florida and Bermuda.*

HABITAT: *Deeper reef waters from 50 to 150 feet deep seem to harbor most of the big Margates, but they do roam the shallow coral patches at times.*

Pigfish
Orthopristis chrysoptera

OTHER NAMES:

Grunt
Orange Grunt
Piggy

RANGE: *South Florida to Cape Hatteras, straggling to New York; also Bermuda.*

HABITAT: *Pigfish are happy in a variety of shallow-water habitats. Most are probably taken over grassy flats.*

DESCRIPTION: The back is gray to blue; sides light tan or whitish. Orange lines and diagonal bars.

SIZE: Common between 3 and 10 inches.

FOOD VALUE: Few large enough to eat, but good.

GAME QUALITIES: Pulls hard against very light rods.

TACKLE AND BAITS: Pigfish rank among the favorite live baits for Seatrout and other species—the thought being that their grunting attracts the predators from a goodly distance away. If you're seeking Pigfish for bait, use canepole or light spinning gear with small hooks and bits of cutbait or shrimp. They are also popular potluck catches from docks.

FISHING SYSTEMS: Drifting; Still Fishing.

Porkfish
Anisotremus virginicus

OTHER NAMES:

Harlequin Grunt
Sisi
Catalineta

RANGE: *South Florida and Bermuda.*

HABITAT: *Coral reefs and inshore coral or shell patches.*

DESCRIPTION: The deep body and bold black markings are reminiscent of the Black Margate, as are the thick lips. Has an overall gold or silvery sheen with two black bars.

SIZE: Averages 8-10 inches; reaches 14 inches or more.

FOOD VALUE: Good.

GAME QUALITIES: Tough battler for its size.

TACKLE AND BAITS: Light spinning and baitcasting outfits; shrimp and cutbaits.

FISHING SYSTEMS: Still Fishing.

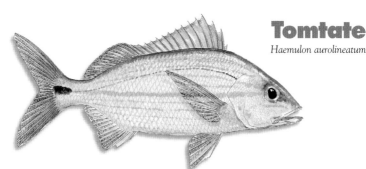

Tomtate
Haemulon aurolineatum

DESCRIPTION: Color is white or silvery, with a prominent gold or brown stripe running from gill to tail. Thinner stripes may also be present. There is a dark blotch just forward of the tail fin.

SIZE: Usually about 6 inches; seldom larger.

FOOD VALUE: Small but good panfish.

GAME QUALITIES: Not big enough to put up much resistance.

TACKLE AND BAITS: Light or ultralight spinning tackle; pieces of shrimp and cut fish or squid.

FISHING SYSTEMS: Still Fishing.

OTHER NAMES:

Brown Grunt
Jeniguano
Cuji

RANGE: *South Florida to Cape Hatteras, straggling to Cape Cod; also Bermuda.*

HABITAT: *Inshore patches and offshore reefs of South Florida and Bermuda; Bahamas; mostly offshore from Central Florida northward.*

White Grunt
Haemulon plumieri

DESCRIPTION: Many are light gray; others much darker. Marked with blue and yellow lines on head.

SIZE: The average is 8-10 inches, but many run 12 inches. World record 6 pounds, 8 ounces.

FOOD VALUE: Very good. The smaller ones usually are served whole as panfish.

GAME QUALITIES: Strong when hooked on light tackle.

TACKLE AND BAITS: Spinning and baitcasting outfits and light saltwater gear. Cutbaits are usually chosen.

FISHING SYSTEMS: Still Fishing; Drifting.

OTHER NAMES:

Gray Grunt
Key West Grunt
Ronco Arara

RANGE: *South Florida to New Jersey; also Bermuda.*

HABITAT: *Likes hard or rocky bottom with scattered coral or shell, from near shore in many areas out to at least 100 feet.*

A colorful and sometimes bewildering variety of potential catches awaits the bottom fisherman in southern waters. Many of these fish are familiar only to anglers working the coral reefs of Florida and Bermuda, although quite a few don't mind roaming much farther north to the Mid-Atlantic states, or even to New England toward the end of a long, hot summer. Some of them are more welcome than others: for instance, the Triggerfishes, which are notorious baitstealers yet make delicious eating — if you manage to catch them. Angelfishes and Parrotfishes are merely rare and gaudy surprises on the end of a line, but the Spadefish — which looks like an Angelfish but isn't — is a common and tasty target for fishermen in several states. And there are numerous other bottom-dwellers down there that the angler often has to take, like it or not.

Chapter

Tropical Reef Fish

Gray Triggerfish

Queen Triggerfish

Ocean Triggerfish

Queen Parrotfish

Blue Parrotfish

Rainbow Parrotfish

Blue Angelfish

French Angelfish

Queen Angelfish

Atlantic Spadefish

Bermuda Chub

Squirrelfish

Bigeye

Spotted Scorpionfish

Sand Tilefish

Tilefish

Gray Triggerfish

Balistes capriscus

OTHER NAMES:

Common Triggerfish

Turbot

RANGE: *South Florida to Cape Hatteras, straggling to New England; also Bermuda.*

HABITAT: *Found mostly on offshore reefs and wrecks from Central Florida northward.*

DESCRIPTION: Triggerfishes — this one and the two to follow—all have long dorsal spikes that, when locked in an erect position, can be folded only by pressing the "trigger," the smallest spine to the rear of the dorsal.

SIZE: Most catches run from a pound or less to perhaps 3 pounds. World record 13 pounds, 9 ounces.

FOOD VALUE: Excellent.

GAME QUALITIES: Tough to hook but very game.

TACKLE AND BAITS: Small hooks are essential, and these are best used, of course, on spinning or light ocean tackle. Triggers bite any sort of cutbait.

FISHING SYSTEMS: Still Fishing; Drifting.

Queen Triggerfish

Balistes vetula

OTHER NAMES:

Painted Triggerfish

Queen Turbot

RANGE: *South Florida to New England.*

HABITAT: *Coral reefs in Florida. Father north on deep banks and dropoffs.*

DESCRIPTION: Over coral reefs, the colors are varied and bright, ranging from blue to green. The mouth is circled in bright blue and two or more blue lines run from snout to pectoral fin.

SIZE: From a couple of pounds to 10 or 12 pounds.

FOOD VALUE: Excellent.

GAME QUALITIES: Tough battler on light tackle.

TACKLE AND BAITS: Spinning, baitcasting and light ocean tackle provide the most sport.

FISHING SYSTEMS: Still Fishing; Drifting.

Ocean Triggerfish
Canthidermis sufflamen

DESCRIPTION: Color is an overall dark gray or black.

SIZE: This is the largest Triggerfish in average size, commonly weighing 4-6 pounds; sometimes topping 10. World record 13 pounds, 8 ounces.

FOOD VALUE: Good but tends to be coarser.

GAME QUALITIES: Strong and stubborn.

TACKLE AND BAITS: Spinning, baitcasting and light ocean tackle. Small hooks and baits are essential. Will bite any sort of cutbait. Also takes jigs, and even flies.

FISHING SYSTEMS: Still Fishing; Drift Fishing.

OTHER NAMES:

Ocean Tally
Turbot
Great Trigger

RANGE: *South Florida to Cape Cod; also Bermuda.*

HABITAT: *Mostly encountered well offshore, near the surface.*

Queen Parrotfish
Scarus vetula

DESCRIPTION: Adult males are deep green with yellow highlights on their scales and fins, and wavy black lines around mouth. Females are drab — usually dull brown with a yellow stripe on the side.

SIZE: Up to 2 feet or so.

FOOD VALUE: Not usually eaten.

GAME QUALITIES: Rarely hooked, but strong.

TACKLE AND BAITS: Not targeted, but hooked once in a while by reef anglers.

FISHING SYSTEMS: Still Fishing.

OTHER NAMES:

Vieja

RANGE: *South Florida and Bermuda.*

HABITAT: *Coral reefs.*

Blue Parrotfish

Scarus coeruleus

OTHER NAMES:

Loro Azul

RANGE: *South Florida to New Jersey; also Bermuda.*

HABITAT: *Coral reefs.*

DESCRIPTION: Adult males are deep blue all over; young males and females are lighter blue, with some yellow on head and dorsal fin.

SIZE: Up to 2 feet or so.

FOOD VALUE: Not usually eaten.

GAME QUALITIES: Big enough to fight vigorously when hooked.

TACKLE AND BAITS: Not targeted, but occasionally hooked over the coral reefs.

FISHING SYSTEMS: Still Fishing.

Rainbow Parrotfish

Scarus guacamaia

OTHER NAMES:

Guacamaya

RANGE: *South Florida and Bermuda.*

HABITAT: *Coral reefs.*

DESCRIPTION: The shoulders of adult males are gold. Scales on the rest of the body are deep green or aqua, ringed in gold, with red streaks or spots around the pectoral fins. Scales of females and small males are mostly green with small patches of gold.

SIZE: Often exceeds 3 feet in length.

FOOD VALUE: Not usually eaten.

GAME QUALITIES: Rarely hooked, but very strong.

TACKLE AND BAITS: Occasionally takes a crustacean bait, such as a piece of lobster.

FISHING SYSTEMS: Still Fishing.

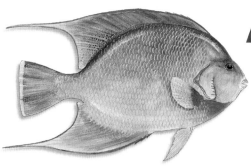

Blue Angelfish
Holacanthus bermudensis

DESCRIPTION: Similar to the Queen Angelfish (with which it possibly hybridizes), but does not have the blue spots on forehead and pectoral. The body is yellowish with blue highlights and blue-tipped dorsal and anal spines. Tail is yellow.

SIZE: Up to about 18 inches.

FOOD VALUE: Fair.

GAME QUALITIES: Rarely hooked, but a brisk fighter.

TACKLE AND BAITS: Not targeted but caught once in a while by reef fishermen on shrimp or cut squid.

FISHING SYSTEMS: Still Fishing.

RANGE: *South Florida to Cape Hatteras, straggling to New York; also Bermuda.*

HABITAT: *Mostly coral reefs in Bermuda and Florida, but also areas with sponges and other marine growth.*

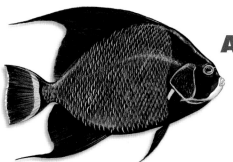

French Angelfish
Pomacanthus paru

DESCRIPTION: A striking fish with black body and yellow-edged scales. A yellow bar also brightens the caudal fin, and more yellow marks the dorsal fin, gill cover and a spot at the base of the pectoral fin.

SIZE: Up to about 15 inches.

FOOD VALUE: Seldom eaten; said to be OK.

GAME QUALITIES: Seldom hooked; spirited fighter.

TACKLE AND BAITS: Caught once in a while by reef fishermen, but feeds mostly on sponges and other marine growth.

FISHING SYSTEMS: Still fishing.

OTHER NAMES:

**Black Angelfish
Cachama Negra
Chirivita**

RANGE: *Florida.*

HABITAT: *Prefers coral reefs and areas with sponges.*

Queen Angelfish

Holacanthus ciliaris

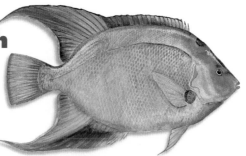

OTHER NAMES:

Isabelita
Cachama
de Piedra

RANGE: *Florida and Bermuda.*

HABITAT: *Prefers coral reefs and areas with plenty of sponges.*

DESCRIPTION: Body is mostly yellow with bright blue markings on the head, and blue edges on the dorsal and anal fins. There is a black spot, ringed with blue, on the forehead, and a dark blue spot at the base of the pectoral fin.

SIZE: Averages 12-18 inches.

FOOD VALUE: Fair.

GAME QUALITIES: Seldom gets a chance to show it, but is a strong fighter for a short period.

TACKLE AND BAITS: Small pieces of shrimp, squid or cut fish will take one occasionally.

FISHING SYSTEMS: Still Fishing.

Atlantic Spadefish

Chaetodipterus faber

OTHER NAMES:

Striped
Angelfish
Chrivita Chiva

RANGE: *South Florida to Cape Cod; also Bermuda.*

HABITAT: *Likes a variety of structure, from mangroves to wrecks.*

DESCRIPTION: The body is very deep and rounded. Superficially similar to Angelfishes, but the divided dorsal, and the color, are giveaways.

SIZE: Averages 2-3 pounds. World record 14 pounds.

FOOD VALUE: Good.

GAME QUALITIES: Difficult to hook, but strong.

TACKLE AND BAITS: Although Spadefish are taken on shrimp, and sometimes on cut fish, they are usually picky biters. Their natural diet is heavy on jellyfish.

FISHING SYSTEMS: Still Fishing.

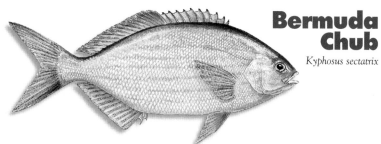

Bermuda Chub

Kyphosus sectatrix

DESCRIPTION: This fish and another species, the **Yellow Chub**, *Kyphosus incisor*, are so nearly identical in appearance and habits that few laymen realize—or care—that two species are involved. The stripes are somewhat more lustrous in the Yellow Chub.

SIZE: Average 2-3 pounds; often exceed 5 pounds. World record 13 pounds, 4 ounces.

FOOD VALUE: Edible but mushy and strong-flavored.

GAME QUALITIES: A very strong fighter.

TACKLE AND BAITS: Chubs are vegetarians, but take cutbaits at times.

FISHING SYSTEMS: Still Fishing; Drift Fishing.

OTHER NAMES:

Sea Chub
Butter Bream
Chopa

RANGE: South Florida to Cape Cod; also Bermuda.

HABITAT: In warm waters, they like reefs and grass patches from near shore to the deep dropoffs. Throughout their range they are also encountered in the open sea, around sargassum weeds.

Squirrelfish

Holocentrus adscensionis

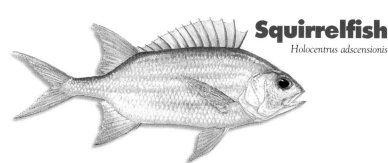

DESCRIPTION: This is a colorful little fellow, but watch out! Its gill covers and dorsal spines are very sharp. The back is red, and the sides show light red or pink stripes on a silvery or white background. The tail is deeply forked and the eye large.

SIZE: Less than a foot.

FOOD VALUE: Edible but hardly worth the effort.

GAME QUALITIES: Hardly any.

TACKLE AND BAITS: Would offer any sport at all only on the lightest of spinning tackle. Hits many cutbaits.

FISHING SYSTEMS: Still Fishing.

OTHER NAMES:

Soldierfish
Candil

RANGE: South Florida to Cape Hatteras; also Bermuda.

HABITAT: Coral reefs and inshore patches in the South; usually on offshore rock or shell bottom off Georgia and the Carolinas.

Bigeye

Priacanthus arenatus

OTHER NAMES:

Toro

Comico

RANGE: *South Florida to Cape Cod; also Bermuda.*

HABITAT: *Coral reefs and rocky areas, usually from 30 feet or so to very deep ledges.*

DESCRIPTION: The compressed body is a solid deep red. The eye and mouth are very large.

SIZE: Less than a foot. World record 6 pounds, 4 ounces.

FOOD VALUE: Pretty good; not much meat.

GAME QUALITIES: Minor.

TACKLE AND BAITS: All sorts of bottom-fishing tackle; small cutbaits.

FISHING SYSTEMS: Still Fishing.

Spotted Scorpionfish

Scorpaena plumieri

OTHER NAMES:

Lionfish

Rosefish

Thornyhead

RANGE: *One or more species may be encountered from Florida to New England.*

HABITAT: *Rough bottom, usually well offshore in states north of Florida, but often on close-in coral patches in Florida and Bermuda.*

DESCRIPTION: Several species occur along the Atlantic Coast, of which the comparatively large Spotted Scorpionfish is one of the most widespread. All have many spikes and some have venomous dorsal spines.

SIZE: Up to a foot. World record 3 pounds, 7 ounces.

FOOD VALUE: Fishermen wisely avoid handling them, but if large enough, they make very good eating.

GAME QUALITIES: None.

TACKLE AND BAITS: Bottom-fishing outfits with cutbaits.

FISHING SYSTEMS: Still Fishing.

Sand Tilefish

Malacanthus plumieri

DESCRIPTION: This is a slender fish with smooth skin and a crescent tail. Color is cream or tan, sometimes with blue highlights. Anal fin extends nearly the length of the underside between ventral fin and tail.

SIZE: Seldom weighs more than a pound or two. World record 2 pounds, 4 ounces.

FOOD VALUE: Pretty good, but seldom eaten; considered a throwback by most fishermen.

GAME QUALITIES: Poor.

TACKLE AND BAITS: Takes any sort of cut fish, plus shrimp and squid; rarely hits a jig. Most are caught by bottom fishermen seeking larger prey.

FISHING SYSTEMS: Still Fishing; Drifting.

OTHER NAMES:

Sand Eel

RANGE: *Occurs as far north as North Carolina and straggles farther, but is most common off the lower Florida coast. Also Bermuda.*

HABITAT: *Sandy bottom, often around edges of coral reefs, mostly from 40 to 150 feet of water.*

Tilefish

Lopholatilus chamaeleonticeps

DESCRIPTION: A fleshy protuberance forward of the dorsal fin, and entirely separate from it, easily identifies the Common Tilefish.

SIZE: Usually 5-10 pounds, but sometimes exceeds 20.

FOOD VALUE: The light, mild flesh is good and commercially popular.

GAME QUALITIES: Poor. Must be taken on heavy gear.

TACKLE AND BAITS: Anglers sometimes use powered reels. Cut fish makes good bait.

FISHING SYSTEMS: Drifting.

OTHER NAMES:

Gray Tilefish
Blue Tilefish
Common Tilefish

RANGE: *South Florida to Nova Scotia.*

HABITAT: *Seldom caught in less than 300 feet and prefers 500 or more. Likes soft bottom with scattered rocks or growth.*

T his catch-all chapter (pardon the pun) looks at a conglomerate of species that usually cause no joy when they turn up on an angler's hook. Some, however, are very good to eat and others are fine gamesters, even though they may not be widely acknowledged as such. But the motley bunch also contains a few, such as the Catfish, that are capable of administering a painful injury, and a couple — certain Puffers — that might even poison you if you don't watch out. Several different fishy families are represented here, and just about the only thing they have in common is that all make good subjects for dockside conversation.

Chapter

A Motley Crew

Atlantic Sturgeon

Shortnose Sturgeon

Goosefish

Ocean Pout

Atlantic Wolffish

Hardhead Catfish

Gafftopsail Catfish

Gulf Toadfish

Atlantic Needlefish

Houndfish

Inshore Lizardfish

Atlantic Cutlassfish

Sharksucker

Remora

Scrawled Cowfish

Bighead Searobin

Northern Puffer

Smooth Puffer

Southern Puffer

Atlantic Sturgeon

Acipenser oxyrhynchus

OTHER NAMES:

Common Sturgeon

RANGE: *From the St. Johns River, Florida, to Labrador.*

HABITAT: *Adults stay in deep water, entering rivers to spawn.*

DESCRIPTION: The Sturgeon looks prehistoric, and its looks are not deceiving. Several rows of bony or shield-like scales run the length of the body, which is dark gray above and whitish on the sides. The snout is long, narrow and upturned.

SIZE: Historically to 15 feet and more than 1,000 pounds. Largest now are probably under 10 feet.

FOOD VALUE: Excellent, but now too depleted to kill.

GAME QUALITIES: Deep fighter; very strong.

TACKLE AND BAITS: Other Sturgeons in the West and Midwest are caught by anglers bottom fishing with cutbaits. Atlantic Sturgeon would take such baits but are now too rare to fish for.

FISHING SYSTEMS: Still Fishing.

Shortnose Sturgeon

Acipenser brevirostrum

OTHER NAMES:

Little Sturgeon

RANGE: *Northern Quebec and New Brunswick to Florida.*

HABITAT: *Stays closer to shore than the Atlantic Sturgeon, preferring river mouths and estuaries; however, it also spawns in fresh water.*

DESCRIPTION: Much smaller than the Atlantic Sturgeon, and further distinguishable by the snout, which is short and rounded.

SIZE: Averages around 2 feet; maximum 4 feet.

FOOD VALUE: Very good, like all Sturgeons.

GAME QUALITIES: Strong, deep fighter.

TACKLE AND BAITS: Any sort of tackle suitable for bottom fishing will do. Clams, squid, shrimp and cut fish all are acceptable baits, but this Sturgeon, too, has been heavily depleted and is seldom caught.

FISHING SYSTEMS: Still Fishing.

Goosefish

Lophius americanus

DESCRIPTION: There's no mistaking a Goosefish, with its huge head, cavernous trapdoor mouth with numerous teeth, and a "fishing pole" atop its head. The latter is the first spine of the dorsal fin, which is flexible and has a "lure" on the end. Small fishes are attracted to the lure and engulfed by the huge mouth.

SIZE: Common at 2 feet or so and 10-15 pounds; grows to at least 50 pounds.

FOOD VALUE: Excellent, despite its appearance.

GAME QUALITIES: Eager striker but not too strong.

TACKLE AND BAITS: Bottom-fishing gear of all sorts.

FISHING SYSTEMS: Still Fishing.

OTHER NAMES:

**Anglerfish
Monkfish**

RANGE: Gulf of St. Lawrence to Florida.

HABITAT: It is common and found from the shallows to the depths in the northern part of its range, but seldom encountered by anglers south of Cape Hatteras, where it stays well offshore all the time.

Ocean Pout

Macrozoarces americanus

DESCRIPTION: Eel-like in appearance. Color is dull yellowish to rusty. Dark markings on sides.

SIZE: Averages 3 pounds; can reach at least 10.

FOOD VALUE: Good but seldom eaten by anglers.

GAME QUALITIES: Not much of a fighter.

TACKLE AND BAITS: Mostly a nuisance. Will take a variety of bottom baits.

FISHING SYSTEMS: Still Fishing; Drifting.

OTHER NAMES:

Eelpout

RANGE: Labrador to Maryland.

HABITAT: From nearshore to deep waters of the continental shelf.

Atlantic Wolffish

Anarhichas lupus

OTHER NAMES:

Ocean Whitefish

RANGE: *Labrador to New Jersey*

HABITAT: *Found from about 30 feet of water to more than 300 feet. Forages for shellfish on hard or rocky bottom.*

DESCRIPTION: Color is dark gray to deep green, with numerous bars on the side. Blunt head with prominent canine teeth, plus crushing teeth in back of mouth. A similar species, the **Spotted Wolffish**, *Anarhicas minor*, has spots instead of bars.

SIZE: Common at 10-15 pounds; grows to 40 or more.

FOOD VALUE: Very good.

GAME QUALITIES: Fairly strong fighter.

TACKLE AND BAITS: Usually taken on bottom-fishing tackle with crab, squid or clam baits.

FISHING SYSTEMS: Still Fishing; Drifting.

Hardhead Catfish

Arius felis

OTHER NAMES:

Marine Catfish
Seacat
Bagre

RANGE: *Florida to Chesapeake Bay. Straggles to New England.*

HABITAT: *Soft-bottom areas of coastal waters, bays, harbors and estuaries.*

DESCRIPTION: Barbels adorn the underside and corners of mouth. Back and upper sides are gray to almost black, with white or silvery underside. Tail is deeply forked. First spines of dorsal and pectoral fins are stiff and sharp and coated with venomous slime that can make a puncture excruciatingly painful.

SIZE: A pound or less on average, but can top 3 pounds.

FOOD VALUE: Good but seldom eaten.

GAME QUALITIES: Gives up after a few hard pulls.

TACKLE AND BAITS: Light tackle of any kind.

FISHING SYSTEMS: Still Fishing; Drift Fishing.

Gafftopsail Catfish

Bagre marinus

DESCRIPTION: The head is bigger and the mouth larger than those of the Hardhead, but coloration is similar. Long, soft streamers extend from the dorsal and pectoral fins.

SIZE: Most specimens run more than 1 pound. Potential could be as high as 10 pounds.

FOOD VALUE: Very good.

GAME QUALITIES: A much better sport fish than the Hardhead. Good for a couple of runs.

TACKLE AND BAITS: Spinning and baitcasting outfits are the ticket. Prefers live small fish.

FISHING SYSTEMS: Still Fishing; Drifting; Casting.

OTHER NAMES:

**Sailcat
Schooner-Rig
Catfish**

RANGE: *Same as the Hardhead, but less numerous*

HABITAT: *Roams more widely throughout the water column in search of food than does the Hardhead. Roams coastal flats but prefers channels and other deep areas. Roams far into rivers.*

Gulf Toadfish

Opsanus beta

DESCRIPTION: Toadfish are well named, with their wide heads, large mouths and warty appearance. Spiny dorsal fins can administer a painful puncture. Sharp gill covers and strong jaws give further reason to handle with care.

SIZE: Less than a foot long.

FOOD VALUE: Poor.

GAME QUALITIES: Strikes hard, but resists feebly.

TACKLE AND BAITS: Never targeted, it usually is caught by bottom fishermen using cutbaits.

FISHING SYSTEMS: Still Fishing.

RANGE: *A pair of closely similar species covers the whole coast. The* **Oyster Toadfish**, ***Opsanus tau*** *is distributed from New England to Florida, where it is joined by the one pictured, the Gulf Toadfish.*

HABITAT: *Rocky areas, usually in shallow water. Well known for its habit of entering discarded cans or any object that is hollow.*

Atlantic Needlefish

Strongylura marina

OTHER NAMES:

Agujon

RANGE: *Nova Scotia to Bermuda and Florida.*

HABITAT: *At home from the open sea to well up coastal streams and into fresh water. They always are at the surface, and on the prowl for slow-sinking baits.*

DESCRIPTION: One or more of several species is familiar to all Atlantic Coast anglers. They are characterized by slender bodies and long, thin bills equipped with many sharp teeth.

SIZE: Usually 1 foot or less; sometimes to 3 feet or so.

FOOD VALUE: Not much there.

GAME QUALITIES: Lots of thrashing.

TACKLE AND BAITS: Ultralight gear could provide a little sport, but anglers try to avoid them. Needlefish will bite any sort of small baits.

FISHING SYSTEMS: Still Fishing; Drifting.

Houndfish

Tylosurus crocodilus

OTHER NAMES:

Giant Needlefish
Gar
Agujon

RANGE: *New York to Florida.*

HABITAT: *Mostly in the open sea, from reef areas out to blue water, but also found near shore over deeper patches and grassbeds.*

DESCRIPTION: Largest of the Needlefish clan, the Houndfish is recognizable by size alone.

SIZE: Averages a yard in length and can top 5 feet. Heavier than needlefish, with weight to 10 pounds.

FOOD VALUE: Quite good, surprisingly.

GAME QUALITIES: Fights like a baby billfish.

TACKLE AND BAITS: A good choice is light spinning gear with small live baitfish or strip baits. They will also hit nearly any artificial lure.

FISHING SYSTEMS: Trolling; Drifting; Still Fishing.

Inshore Lizardfish

Synodus foetens

DESCRIPTION: The Inshore Lizardfish, shown here, is the more familiar of two principal species. The **Offshore Lizardfish**, *Synodus poeyi* sticks to the depths. Both are colored in shades of brown with dark blotches or diamond marks on the sides.

SIZE: The Inshore Lizardfish commonly runs from 12 to 18 inches. The Offshore variety is smaller.

FOOD VALUE: Poor. The meat is white but very bony.

GAME QUALITIES: Too small to fight much.

TACKLE AND BAITS: Lizardfish are strictly nuisances that horn in on baits intended for other fish.

FISHING SYSTEMS: Still Fishing; Drift Fishing.

OTHER NAMES:

Snakefish
Galliwasp
Lagarto
Sand Pike

RANGE: Massachusetts to Florida.

HABITAT: Both types prefer soft bottom, with the Inshore variety being found from the coastline out to about 50 feet.

Atlantic Cutlassfish

Trichiurus lepturus

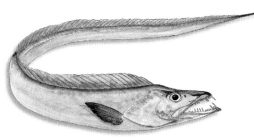

DESCRIPTION: Body is flat, thin and silver. The dorsal fin runs the length of the back, but there is no tail fin — only a whip-like filament. The mouth is large and menacing, with many fang-like teeth.

SIZE: Average is about 2 feet, with an occasional one running as long as 4 feet or so.

FOOD VALUE: Poor. Little meat and quite bony.

GAME QUALITIES: A lightweight with little fight.

TACKLE AND BAITS: Usually caught on tackle scaled for Mackerel and Bluefish.

FISHING SYSTEMS: Still Fishing; Drifting; Trolling.

OTHER NAMES:

Ribbonfish

RANGE: Massachusetts to Florida.

HABITAT: Open coastal waters, plus bays, inlets and coastal streams. Often found in company with Bluefish or Spanish Mackerel.

Sharksucker

Echeneis naucrates

OTHER NAMES:

Remora

RANGE: *Nova Scotia to Florida; also Bermuda.*

HABITAT: *Wanders both off-shore and inshore waters.*

DESCRIPTION: This is the most familiar of several closely related "hitchhiking" fishes of the Atlantic Coast, not only because of wider distribution, but also because it uses a greater variety of hosts, including turtles and marine mammals. The other Remoras generally each stick to one type of host.

SIZE: Usually 1 foot or less, but can exceed 3 feet.

FOOD VALUE: Poor.

GAME QUALITIES: Not a bad fighter on light tackle.

TACKLE AND BAITS: Never targeted, but often caught on all sorts of gear and any kind of natural bait.

FISHING SYSTEMS: Drift Fishing; Still Fishing.

Remora

Remora remora

OTHER NAMES:

Sharksucker

RANGE: *Nova Scotia to Florida, but less often caught than the Sharksucker.*

HABITAT: *Free-roaming, usually offshore. Attaches mainly to Sharks.*

DESCRIPTION: This species is solid in color—usually gray or charcoal—and lacks the stripe of the preceding type. It also has a rounder head.

SIZE: From a few inches to a couple of feet.

FOOD VALUE: Nil.

GAME QUALITIES: Not much fight.

TACKLE AND BAITS: Never targeted, but often caught on all sorts of gear and any kind of natural bait it can swallow.

FISHING SYSTEMS: Drift Fishing; Still Fishing.

Scrawled Cowfish
Lactophrys quadricornis

DESCRIPTION: This is the most familiar of several species, all of which have a smooth skin, small mouth and box-like shape, which is due to a covering of tank-like armor just under the skin — an external skeleton, so to speak.

SIZE: Usually a foot or less, but can exceed 18 inches.

FOOD VALUE: Said to have excellent meat inside its armor, but also said to be toxic at times.

ANGLING VALUE: They are baitstealers which occasionally get hooked on small rigs.

TACKLE AND BAITS: Spinning with live or dead shrimp.

FISHING SYSTEMS: Still Fishing.

OTHER NAMES:

Trunkfish
Boxfish

RANGE: *New England to Florida, but most common in the southern part of the range and in Bermuda.*

HABITAT: *Strictly bottom dwelling. Likes grassy or shell-strewn areas.*

Bighead Searobin
Prionotus tribulus

DESCRIPTION: These fish get their names from the wing-like pectoral fins, the forward rays of which are modified into "feet" that they use to creep along the bottom. Again, several species are present in our range. This one and the **Northern Searobin,** *Prionotus carolinus* turn up most often.

SIZE: Usually a foot or less.

FOOD VALUE: Tasty, but usually tossed back.

GAME QUALITIES: None.

TACKLE AND BAITS: Usually taken accidentally by bottom fishermen on small cutbaits.

FISHING SYSTEMS: Still Fishing; Drifting.

RANGE: *The Bighead is found from New England to South Florida; the Carolina from Nova Scotia to North Florida.*

HABITAT: *Prefers soft or muddy bottom.*

Northern Puffer

Sphoeroides maculatus

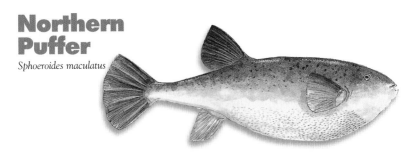

OTHER NAMES:

Blowfish
Swellfish
Toadfish
Sea Squab

RANGE: Newfoundland to North Florida.

HABITAT: Usually prefer calm and protected water, but are not picky about type of bottom.

DESCRIPTION: The back is dark gray or green with small black spots. Underside is white and, when inflated, rough. Most distinguishing features are dark bars on the sides. The small mouth is equipped with large, clipping teeth.

SIZE: Average is 8-10 inches.

FOOD VALUE: Excellent if properly cleaned. Widely marketed as "Sea Squab" and, unlike other puffers, not considered poisonous (see Introduction).

GAME QUALITIES: Poor.

TACKLE AND BAITS: All sorts of cut fish.

FISHING SYSTEMS: Still Fishing.

Smooth Puffer

Lagocephalus laevigatus

OTHER NAMES:

Silver Puffer
Rabbitfish

RANGE: New England to Florida.

HABITAT: Basically an offshore fish that's caught by anglers only when it comes to the beaches, or into bays, at unpredictable times.

DESCRIPTION: Dark gray back with silver sides and belly. No markings. The skin is smooth except for the belly, which is "goose-pimpled."

SIZE: Averages 2 pounds and can reach 6 pounds or so.

FOOD VALUE: Provides more meat and just as good as the other Puffers, but should be cleaned with care.

GAME QUALITIES: Can put up a good fight.

TACKLE AND BAITS: Any kind of outfit suitable for bottom fishing, the lighter the better.

FISHING SYSTEMS: Still Fishing.

Southern Puffer

Sphoeroides nephelus

DESCRIPTION: Mottled yellow or brown with yellowish or white underside. Markings are circular. Mouth is small but with protruding human-like teeth that can nip a chunk out of a careless angler. Their bellies are rough when inflated.

SIZE: Averages less than a foot.

FOOD VALUE: Excellent. Unfortunately, however, improper cleaning can lead to serious, even fatal, poisoning. Best eat something else.

GAME QUALITIES: Not much.

TACKLE AND BAITS: As long-suffering inshore anglers know, Blowfish will hit many kinds of lures, generally ruining those made of plastic or hair. They will take any sort of natural bait as well, and the few people who go after them for food use small hooks baited with dabs of shrimp, squid or cut fish. No sport on any tackle.

FISHING SYSTEMS: Still Fishing; Drifting; Casting.

OTHER NAMES:

Blowfish
Toadfish
Swellfish

RANGE: Florida.

HABITAT: At home in many shallow habitats. Usually prefers protected water but also found around jetties, where it is sheltered by the rocks.

The Common Eel is a gourmet treat for some folks but, as a rule, Eels of any kind are more likely to elicit shudders than praise from American fishermen. The Conger is a frequent target in Great Britain because few other really large sea fish are available there, but on our side of the Atlantic few anglers deliberately go after them, despite their large size potential. Even so, the Conger stands higher on the popularity scale than do Morays, which nobody ever cares to haul into their boat.

The Eels

Conger Eel

American Eel

Green Moray

Spotted Moray

Conger Eel

Conger oceanicus

OTHER NAMES:

American Conger

RANGE: *Nova Scotia to North Florida; most plentiful from Cape Cod to Cape Hatteras.*

HABITAT: *Like other Eels it sticks to cover, but is at home either in the ocean depths or near shore, where it is frequently caught around docks, piers and jetties.*

DESCRIPTION: Although usually larger and stouter than the Common Eel, the Conger could be confused with it when small. One distinguishing feature is the dorsal fin of the Conger, which begins above the pectoral fin — much farther forward than that of the Common Eel. Also, the lower jaw of the Conger is shorter than the upper. Color is dark gray or brown, with a tan or whitish belly.

SIZE: Commonly reaches weights of 20 pounds or more. The maximum potential is possibly as much as 100 pounds.

FOOD VALUE: Not bad but not popular.

GAME QUALITIES: Larger specimens are very tough — at least until the angler gets them moving off the bottom.

TACKLE AND BAITS: Stout rods and fairly strong lines, to 30- or 40-pound-test, may be needed to yank a big Conger from its hiding place. Small live fish, squid, crabs or cutbaits all are acceptable.

FISHING SYSTEMS: Still Fishing.

American Eel

Anguilla rostrata

DESCRIPTION: Color is dingy brown or olive above, yellowish on belly. The dorsal fin starts well behind the pectoral fins and combines with the caudal and anal fins to make one continuous fin that runs all the way to the vent.

SIZE: Averages 2 feet or so; reaches at least 4 feet and 8 pounds. World record 9 pounds, 4 ounces.

FOOD VALUE: Esteemed by some people, but difficult to handle and clean. "Slippery as an eel" is not a figure of speech.

GAME QUALITIES: Not much of a puller; more of a twister.

TACKLE AND BAITS: Caught mostly by bottom-fishing at night. Will take all the popular fish and shellfish baits.

OTHER NAMES:

Common Eel

RANGE: *Nova Scotia to Florida.*

HABITAT: *The Eel is anadromous and more commonly encountered in fresh water, but is sometimes caught in estuaries and river mouths. Hides during the day under rocks or other cover. Forages at night.*

Green Moray

Gymnothorax funebris

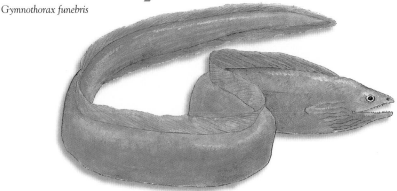

RANGE: *Most common off Florida and Bermuda, but is encountered along most of the Atlantic Coast to New England.*

HABITAT: *Both inshore and in deep water, wherever there are holes or crevices, such as around rocks, coral reefs, jetties, pilings or wrecks.*

DESCRIPTION: This is the largest of the Morays. Color is solid overall and ranges from pale lime to bright green. Morays have no pectoral fins and are further distinguished from Congers by the compressed body, bigger mouth and longer teeth.

SIZE: Averages 3-5 feet and can exceed 7 feet. World record 33 pounds, 8 ounces.

FOOD VALUE: Edible, but unappetizing at best, and also implicated in Ciguatera poisoning (see Introduction).

GAME QUALITIES: Tough to pull out of its hole, but its biggest fight comes after landing, when it likes to tie itself—and the fishing line—into knots. Best for the angler to cut the line as a Moray can administer a serious and infectious bite.

TACKLE AND BAITS: Never targeted, it's usually caught on bottom-fishing tackle of various sorts, baited with live baitfish or cutbait.

FISHING SYSTEMS: Still Fishing.

Spotted Moray

Gymnothorax moringa

DESCRIPTION: White or yellowish with many dark spots that vary in size. Like other Morays, it has two sets of nostrils, the ones on the tip of the nose being protrusive and tubular in shape.

SIZE: Common at 1-2 feet; seldom longer than 3 feet.

FOOD VALUE: Minimal.

GAME QUALITIES: None. Most are caught on tackle selected with much heavier and more coveted prizes in mind.

TACKLE AND BAITS: The catch usually comes as a surprise—and not a very welcome surprise—while bottom-fishing with cutbaits.

FISHING SYSTEMS: Still Fishing.

RANGE: *Cape Hatteras southward; most often seen off Florida and Bermuda.*

HABITAT: *Prefers clear water, but might be found from close inshore out to the deep reefs. Like its relatives, it sticks to the nooks and crannies.*

Journalism and literature have long presented Sharks as vicious man-eaters. Some are, of course, but in real life it is mostly the other way around. Sharks are so valuable in the market that the future of many species is in doubt. In the sportfishing world, their reviews have long been mixed, with a few species given high praise as gamefish, and others looked upon as time-wasting nuisances. The biggest difference, naturally, is size, and when it comes to size, the Shark family has it in spades. The Great White Shark is the largest predatory fish in the ocean, and several other kinds often weigh half a ton or more. In any size, however, Sharks are generally strong and speedy fighters, and some of them get off spectacular jumps.

Chapter

The Sharks

Atlantic Sharpnose Shark
Blacktip Shark
Blue Shark
Bonnethead
Bull Shark
Dusky Shark
Great Hammerhead
Lemon Shark
Nurse Shark
Oceanic Whitetip Shark
Porbeagle
Reef Shark
Sandbar Shark
Scalloped Hammerhead
Shortfin Mako
Silky Shark
Smooth Dogfish
Smooth Hammerhead
Spiny Dogfish
Spinner Shark
Thresher Shark
Tiger Shark
White Shark

Atlantic Sharpnose Shark

Rhizoprionodon terraenovae

RANGE: *South Florida to South Carolina; straying north to New England.*

HABITAT: *Sticks to coastal waters—surf, bays and river mouths, often in schools.*

DESCRIPTION: The snout is longer than the mouth is wide. Color is brown or dark gray above and white below. Pale white spots may be scattered over the dorsal surface in large specimens. Dorsal and caudal fins are edged in black.

SIZE: A small Shark, averaging less than 10 pounds. World record 16 pounds.

FOOD VALUE: Very good.

GAME QUALITIES: Strong on very light gear.

TACKLE AND BAITS: Best choices are light spinning and baitcasting outfits. Small live or dead baitfish.

FISHING SYTEMS: Still Fishing; Drifting.

Blacktip Shark

Carcharhinus limbatus

OTHER NAMES:

Spinner Shark
Small
Blacktip Shark

RANGE: *Cape Cod to South Florida.*

HABITAT: *Found anywhere from the deep sea to shorelines and bays. Also plentiful around many inlets.*

DESCRIPTION: Tips of the dorsal and pectoral fins are black, as is the lower lobe of the caudal fin.

SIZE: Common from 5-30 pounds. World record 270 pounds, 9 ounces.

FOOD VALUE: Very good.

GAME QUALITIES: Pound for pound, probably the scrappiest of sharks. Wages a wild battle on light tackle.

TACKLE AND BAITS: Spinning, baitcasting and even fly casting are popular approaches in Florida, because Blacktips will hit a variety of artificial lures and baits.

FISHING SYSTEMS: Casting; Drifting; Still Fishing.

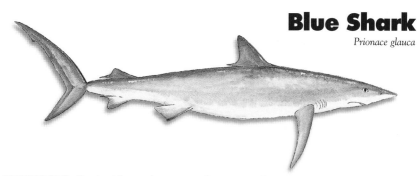

Blue Shark
Prionace glauca

DESCRIPTION: Bright blue color, pointed snout and extra-long dorsal fins make this shark easy to pick out.

SIZE: Averages 100-300 pounds. World record 454 pounds.

FOOD VALUE: Fair.

GAME QUALITIES: Rather poor compared to many.

TACKLE AND BAITS: Most Blue Sharks are caught by chumming with whole or cut fish on ocean tackle.

FISHING SYSTEMS: Drifting; Trolling.

OTHER NAMES:

**Blue Dogfish
Blue Whaler**

RANGE: *Nova Scotia to South Florida.*

HABITAT: *Commonly found near the surface in the temperate zone, but usually stays very deep in warm-water areas.*

Bonnethead
Sphyrna tiburo

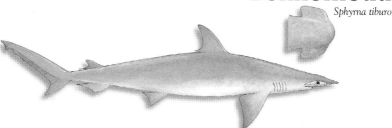

DESCRIPTION: The head is rounded or shovel-shaped, rather than elongated as with other Hammerheads.

SIZE: Averages 2-5 pounds; occasionally tops 10 pounds and can reach 20 or so. World record 23 pounds, 11 ounces.

FOOD VALUE: Good.

GAME QUALITIES: A spirited fighter on light tackle.

TACKLE AND BAITS: Light spinning and baitcasting outfits. Will take virtually any sort of small live fish, shrimp or cutbait.

FISHING SYSTEMS: Drifting; Still Fishing.

OTHER NAMES:

**Bonnet Shark
Shovelnose
Shark**

RANGE: *South Florida to Cape Hatteras, straggling to New England.*

HABITAT: *Found mostly inshore, but roams from shallow flats to deep channels and bays.*

Bull Shark
Carcharhinus leucas

OTHER NAMES:

Freshwater Shark

Cub Shark

RANGE: *South Florida to Cape Hatteras; straggles north to New York.*

HABITAT: *Inhabits both offshore and nearshore waters and sometimes roams far into freshwater streams.*

DESCRIPTION: Similar to the Sandbar Shark but has a shorter, wider snout. It has a large first dorsal fin, starting above the middle of the pectoral fin, and a much smaller second dorsal.

SIZE: Can exceed 10 feet and 400 pounds, but most run 6-8 feet and 100-300 pounds. World record 490 pounds.

FOOD VALUE: Good.

GAME QUALITIES: A rugged fighter.

TACKLE AND BAITS: Although more appropriately matched to medium ocean outfits, the Bull is a pet target of adventurous casters in the Florida Keys.

FISHING SYSTEMS: Still Fishing; Drifting.

Dusky Shark
Carcharhinus obscurus

OTHER NAMES:

Ground Shark

Sand Shark

RANGE: *South Florida to Cape Cod; rarely to Newfoundland in summer.*

HABITAT: *Primarily coastal, from beaches to the edge of the continental shelf.*

DESCRIPTION: Distinguished from similar species such as the Sandbar Shark by a ridge between the dorsal fins.

SIZE: Most catches are 8 to 10 feet long, with weights up to 250 pounds. World record 764 pounds.

FOOD VALUE: Good.

GAME QUALITIES: A good fighter, but not ranked with the Mako for gameness.

TACKLE AND BAITS: Medium to heavy ocean outfits; go lighter at your own risk.

FISHING SYSTEMS: Still Fishing; Drift Fishing.

Great Hammerhead

Sphyrna mokarran

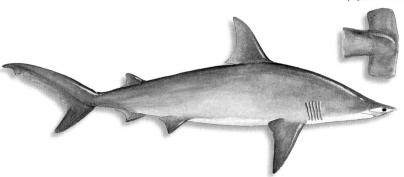

DESCRIPTION: Easily distinguished from other Hammerheads by size alone, but if confusion exists, note that the frontal edge of the Great One's "hammer" is not rounded, but flat. Also, it is the only Hammerhead in which the rear edge of the pelvic fin is curved.

SIZE: Many specimens exceed 500 pounds and some reach twice that weight. Maximum could be as much as one ton. World record 991 pounds.

FOOD VALUE: Seldom eaten.

GAME QUALITIES: Sheer size makes it a formidable opponent.

TACKLE AND BAITS: Only the heaviest sporting gear stands much of a chance—130-pound line or, at the least, 80-pound. Will take large fresh-dead baitfish, but is more easily hooked on oversize live bait.

FISHING SYSTEMS: Drifting; Still Fishing; Trolling.

OTHER NAMES:

Giant Hammerhead

RANGE: *Seen mostly off Florida and Bermuda, but wanders as far as Cape Hatteras in the summer.*

HABITAT: *Usually the open sea, but not uncommon close to the beaches or in large inlets.*

Lemon Shark

Negaprion brevirostris

OTHER NAMES:

Brown Shark

RANGE: *South Florida to South Carolina; wandering past Cape Hatteras to New York in summer.*

HABITAT: *Does most of its feeding in the shallows, along shorelines and over flats, but also likes deeper bay waters, channels, and river mouths. Does not roam far offshore.*

DESCRIPTION: Color is brown with a yellowish cast to the underside. The first dorsal fin is short and not much larger than the second dorsal. The pectorals are triangular and wide.

SIZE: Maximum is around 10 feet and 400 pounds. World record 405 pounds.

FOOD VALUE: Good.

GAME QUALITIES: Not a jumper like the Blacktip, but a strong fighter and popular target.

TACKLE AND BAITS: Like the Blacktip, the Lemon will take a variety of live and dead natural baits, and also artificial lures that are carefully and properly presented.

FISHING SYSTEMS: Casting; Drifting; Still Fishing.

Nurse Shark

Ginglymostoma cirratum

RANGE: *Cape Hatteras to South Florida, where it is most common.*

HABITAT: *Frequently sighted on shallow flats of South Florida and the Keys, where it usually is lying still. Also lies still in deeper water under reef and rock ledges, and around navigation markers.*

DESCRIPTION: Color is much like that of the Lemon but is easy to distinguish by its underslung mouth and barbels at the nostrils.

SIZE: In shallow water, most run from 5 to 50 pounds, World record 210 pounds.

FOOD VALUE: Excellent.

GAME QUALITIES: Probably the worst of all Sharks.

TACKLE AND BAIT: In shallow water, even the lightest kinds of tackle will handle a Nurse shark.

FISHING SYSTEMS: Still Fishing.

Oceanic Whitetip Shark

Carcharhinus longimanus

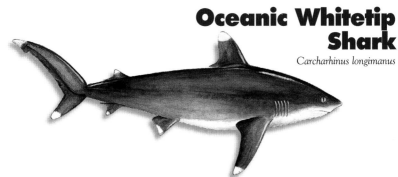

DESCRIPTION: Easily spotted by the glaring white tips of the dorsal, pectoral and caudal fins. Even without the white (and it's absent on a rare specimen) the high, rounded dorsal and long, rounded pectoral fins are giveaways.

SIZE: To 10 feet and 150 pounds. World record 369.

FOOD VALUE: Good.

GAME QUALITIES: An excellent battler on light tackle.

TACKLE AND BAITS: Light to medium ocean tackle, with lines to 30-pound test.

FISHING SYSTEMS: Drifting; Trolling.

OTHER NAMES:

Whitetip Shark

RANGE: *New England to South Florida.*

HABITAT: *Sticks almost entirely to the deep blue ocean.*

Porbeagle

Lamna nasus

DESCRIPTION: Closely related and similar in appearance to the Mako and Great White Sharks, the Porbeagle's most obvious distinguishing feature is a white patch on the rear lower edge of the main dorsal fin.

SIZE: Averages 100-200 pounds. World record 507.

FOOD VALUE: Good.

GAME QUALITIES: One of the best Sharks for fight.

TACKLE AND BAITS: Schooling types of fishes such as Mackerel, Herring and Bonito make the best baits.

FISHING SYSTEMS: Drifting; Trolling.

OTHER NAMES:

Mackerel Shark
Bonito Shark

RANGE: *Labrador to New York, straggling to Cape Hatteras.*

HABITAT: *Open ocean; occasionally ventures near shore.*

Reef Shark

Carcharhinus perezi

OTHER NAMES:

Caribbean
Reef Shark

RANGE: *South Florida; straying to South Carolina.*

HABITAT: *Found widely from reefs to surf and bays.*

DESCRIPTION: Difficult to tell from the Dusky Shark, but the body is fatter, the gill slits smaller, and the trailing edge of the ventral fin is indented. Color is gray or tan above, yellowish below.

SIZE: Few reach 100 pounds; most run 30-40 pounds.

FOOD VALUE: Good.

GAME QUALITIES: A zippy fighter, but usually small and considered a nuisance by most anglers.

TACKLE AND BAITS: Spinning, baitcasting and light ocean outfits. Small dead fish and cutbaits work well.

FISHING SYSTEMS: Still Fishing; Drift Fishing.

Sandbar Shark

Carcharhinus plumbeus

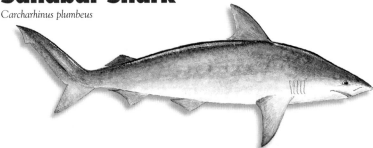

OTHER NAMES:

Sand Shark
Brown Shark

RANGE: *New England to South Florida; most common south of Cape Hatteras.*

HABITAT: *Mostly inshore and around beaches; also in bays and channels. Doesn't mind murky water.*

DESCRIPTION: Distinctive features are the wide, triangular dorsal and pectoral fins. The dorsal is situated almost directly above the pectoral. Color ranges from gray to brown above, whitish below.

SIZE: Averages 50-100 pounds. World record 260.

FOOD VALUE: Good.

GAME QUALITIES: A fine battler on lighter tackle.

TACKLE AND BAITS: Heavy spinning and baitcasting outfits; surf rods. Chunks of fresh dead fish.

FISHING SYSTEMS: Still Fishing; Drifting.

Scalloped Hammerhead

Sphyrna lewini

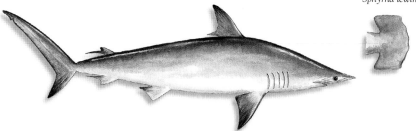

DESCRIPTION: Pectoral fin has dark tip on underside. Front edge of "hammer" is slightly rounded.

SIZE: Averages 75 pounds. World record 335.

FOOD VALUE: Good.

GAME QUALITIES: Runs are fast and strong.

TACKLE AND BAITS: Since it is a middleweight, it makes a good candidate for medium tackle.

FISHING SYSTEMS: Drifting; Still Fishing.

RANGE: *New Jersey southward; common from Cape Hatteras to South Florida; also Bermuda.*

HABITAT: *Open ocean, but commonly roams close to the beaches and sometimes into large bays.*

Shortfin Mako

Isurus oxyrinchus

DESCRIPTION: Makos have bulging teeth which differ from those of other well-known sharks in being long, narrow and pointed, rather than v-shaped. A similar species, the **Longfin Mako, *Isurus paucus*** is only rarely caught.

SIZE: Usual range is 200-600 pounds. World record 1,115.

FOOD VALUE: Excellent.

GAME QUALITIES: A very strong and vicious fighter that often gets off high, spectacular leaps.

TACKLE AND BAITS: Best to choose ocean tackle, in at least the 30-pound line class, with 50-pound and 80-pound lines needed to handle the big ones.

FISHING SYSTEMS: Trolling; Drift Fishing.

OTHER NAMES:

Blue Pointer

RANGE: *New England to South Florida; more common in the South.*

HABITAT: *The open sea. Shortfin Makos frequently cruise, and strike, at the surface, whereas the Longfin is almost entirely a deep dweller.*

Silky Shark

Carcharhinus falciformis

OTHER NAMES:

Wharf Shark

RANGE: *New Jersey to South Florida, where it is most common.*

HABITAT: *The open sea, sometimes venturing to coastal waters.*

DESCRIPTION: Color is silky brown or bronze above, white below. The shape is rather slender. The snout is short and slender. The first dorsal is comparatively small and begins at a point behind the pectoral fin.

SIZE: Usually 30-100 pounds, but not rare at 300 pounds. World record 762.

FOOD VALUE: Good.

GAME QUALITIES: Very rugged on suitable tackle.

TACKLE AND BAITS: Light classes of ocean tackle, plus heavy spinning and baitcasting gear with cut baits.

FISHING SYSTEMS: Drift Fishing.

Smooth Dogfish

Mustelus canis

OTHER NAMES:

Common Dogfish
Grayfish

RANGE: *Nova Scotia to South Florida.*

HABITAT: *Both shallow and deep water; mostly deep water south of Charleston.*

DESCRIPTION: Similar in appearance to the Spiny Dogfish, but lacks the spots and the spines. Also, the second dorsal is almost as large as the first, and the teeth are small and round.

SIZE: Averages 2 or 3 feet; sometimes to 4 feet. World record 26 pounds, 12 ounces.

FOOD VALUE: Very Good.

GAME QUALITIES: Considered a nuisance.

TACKLE AND BAITS: Sporty only on light gear, such as spinning and baitcasting outfits.

FISHING SYSTEMS: Still Fishing; Drifting.

Smooth Hammerhead

Sphyrna zygaena

DESCRIPTION: Size and habits are similar to those of the Scalloped Hammerhead, and few anglers make any distinction. The head is very slightly rounded, but with no central indentation.

SIZE: Averages around 100 pounds; can top 200. World record 363 pounds.

FOOD VALUE: Good.

GAME QUALITIES: Fast and strong, but no great shakes for stamina.

TACKLE AND BAITS: Like the Scalloped Hammerhead, it is a good candidate for lighter tackle, and takes the same baits.

FISHING SYSTEMS: Drifting; Still Fishing.

RANGE: *Nova Scotia to South Florida.*

HABITAT: *Northern part of range in summer; southern in winter. Roams the open sea, with occasional forays into shallower water. Commonly seen at the surface by offshore anglers.*

Spiny Dogfish

Squalus acanthias

DESCRIPTION: Brownish gray above, light gray below. Scattered light spots on sides. Second dorsal fin is smaller than the first dorsal, but each is fitted with a sharp spike on the forward edge that can administer a painful stab to the incautious angler.

SIZE: Averages 2 or 3 feet; seldom exceeds 4 feet. World Record 15 pounds, 12 ounces.

FOOD VALUE: Very good.

GAME QUALITIES: Poor.

TACKLE AND BAITS: Sporty only on light gear, such as spinning and baitcasting outfits.

FISHING SYSTEMS: Still Fishing; Drifting.

OTHER NAMES:

Pike Shark
Grayfish

RANGE: *Labrador to Cape Hatteras, straying to North Florida in winter.*

HABITAT: *Travels in large packs from close inshore to 500 feet or more, and at all water levels.*

Spinner Shark

Carcharhinus brevipinna

OTHER NAMES:

Large Blacktip Shark

RANGE: *North Carolina to South Florida.*

HABITAT: *The open sea, but it often roams toward shore in southern Florida where the Gulf Stream is close to land.*

DESCRIPTION: The black-tipped fins fool many anglers into believing the Spinner and the Blacktip Sharks are the same species. The coloration is also similar, except that the Spinner has a whitish or light gray band on its lower sides.

SIZE: Common from 10-50 pounds. World record 190.

FOOD VALUE: Very good.

GAME QUALITIES: A spectacular fighter on light tackle.

TACKLE AND BAITS: Best choices are medium to heavy spinning tackle and light ocean gear.

FISHING SYSTEMS: Casting; Drifting; Still Fishing.

Thresher Shark

Alopias vulpinus

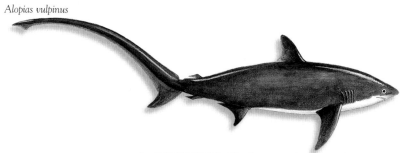

RANGE: *Newfoundland to South Florida; usually inshore in the North and offshore in the South.*

HABITAT: *The deep sea; sometimes seen at the surface but almost always caught far under it.*

DESCRIPTION: The long, scythe-like tail is a dead giveaway. A similar and rarer species, the **Bigeye Thresher**, *Alopias superciliosus* is distinguished by its huge eye.

SIZE: Average is 250-350 pounds; both grow to perhaps 1,000 pounds. World record 767 pounds, 3 ounces.

FOOD VALUE: Good.

GAME QUALITIES: An excellent fighter.

TACKLE AND BAIT: Heavy classes of ocean tackle. Most are caught by deep drifting, but in northern waters they may be taken by trolling or visual baiting.

FISHING SYSTEMS: Drift Fishing; Trolling.

Tiger Shark
Galeocerdo cuvieri

DESCRIPTION: Color is dark above, yellowish below, with dark markings. On smaller specimens, the markings take the shape of spots—hence the name "Leopard." The big ones become "Tigers" as the spots grow and blend together into stripes. The patterns do vary.

SIZE: The largest Shark likely to be encountered. Quite a few 1,000-pounders have been taken. World record 1,780 pounds.

FOOD VALUE: Small ones good.

GAME QUALITIES: Not spectacular but very strong.

TACKLE AND BAITS: The heaviest sporting outfits are required for adult Tigers.

FISHING SYSTEMS: Still Fishing; Drifting.

OTHER NAMES:

Leopard Shark

RANGE: *New England to South Florida, but far more common in warm water.*

HABITAT: *The open sea, primarily, but many—including some giants—come close to the beaches, and even into bays.*

White Shark
Carcharodon carcharias

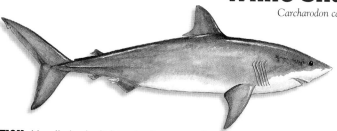

DESCRIPTION: Usually looks lighter in the water than other big sharks, although the actual color varies from overall grayish white to brownish above and white below. In shape it is much like the Mako.

SIZE: Largest of all predatory Sharks, recorded to 20 feet and 2 tons. World record 2,664 pounds.

FOOD VALUE: Probably fair to good, but seldom eaten.

GAME QUALITIES: Among the ultimate challenges.

TACKLE AND BAITS: Heaviest tackle available.

FISHING SYSTEMS: Drift Fishing; Still Fishing.

OTHER NAMES:

Great White Shark

White Pointer

RANGE: *Newfoundland to South Florida. Not common anywhere, but most likely to be encountered in temperate waters.*

HABITAT: *The open sea, although it sometimes ventures to the beaches and even into coastal streams.*

Rays and Skates, along with the related Torpedo and Guitarfish, are cousins to the Sharks, and are found in virtually every Atlantic Coast habitat, from the deep sea to well inside many coastal rivers. For the most part, anglers try to ignore them but that's a difficult goal to achieve, especially for those who fish natural baits on the bottom. These do pull hard for a short while and are adept at plastering their wide bodies to the bottom to resist lifting, but they are nearly always a disappointment to their captors, who are expecting something more prestigious. What's worse, some are dangerous. The Skates and Rays covered here were selected as being the ones most familiar to fishermen, in both northern and southern waters of the Atlantic Coast. Veteran saltwater anglers are also acquainted with Manta Rays, Eagle Rays and other wandering types which are not included here because they rarely end up on a line unless accidentally snagged.

Rays and Skates

Southern Stingray

Dasyatis americana

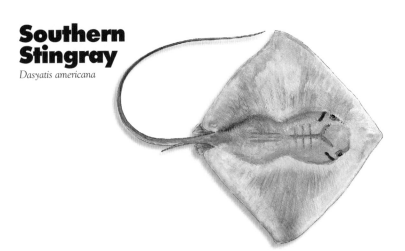

OTHER NAMES:

Stingaree

RANGE: *Florida to New Jersey, straggling northward.*

HABITAT: *Both species forage on soft bottom, particularly flats and shorelines.*

DESCRIPTION: Recreational fishermen generally care little about differentiating among the species that are included under this common name. The two most familiar ones are the pictured **Southern Stingray, Dasyatis americana**, and the smaller **Atlantic Stingray, Dasyatis sabina**, which differs only slightly in appearance, with a more pointed "nose" and more rounded "wingtips." Both are dark colored and stand out vividly when moving and "mudding" on flats, or just off shallow beaches and shorelines. But they can hide in the sand or mud as well, so take care if wading! Unlike the Skates, Stingrays are all equipped with dangerous barbed spikes on their tails.

SIZE: Usually 2-3 feet in "wingspan," although individuals can run at least twice that size. World record 246 pounds.

FOOD VALUE: Few anglers care to bring them in, but the "wings" and back are quite good, tasting much like scallops.

GAME QUALITIES: Not great fighters. Their runs can be initially strong but are usually rather short. Their tactic of sticking to the bottom like a suction cup, however, can work up an angler's sweat.

TACKLE AND BAITS: All kinds of tackle, since most are caught accidentally. Should you wish to target a Stingray along the shore or on the flats, try spinning tackle baited with shrimp or crab. From a pier or bridge, use heavier gear—maybe surf tackle—with the same sort of bait.

FISHING SYSTEMS: Still Fishing.

Roughtail Stingray

Dasyatis centroura

DESCRIPTION: The barbed spike is long, and there also are numerous spines along the tail, back and shoulders. The Roughtail grows much larger than the two Stingrays named earlier, but is similar in color and general shape.

SIZE: Averaging around 4 feet, its "wingspan" exceeds 6 feet at times. Overall length can top 10 feet. World record 405 pounds.

FOOD VALUE: Good.

GAME QUALITIES: Basically the same as smaller Rays, but most specimens are much larger, and so much tougher to handle.

TACKLE AND BAITS: Not targeted, they usually are hooked on rather heavy bottom-fishing outfits by fishermen seeking popular groundfish. They will eat just about any sort of fish or shellfish bait, both live and cut.

FISHING SYSTEMS: Still Fishing.

OTHER NAMES:

Northern
  Stingray
Stingaree

RANGE: This is primarily a northern species, most often seen off New England, New York and the Mid-Atlantic states. It does, however, wander southward as far as Central Florida.

HABITAT: Encountered from the shore to deep offshore banks.

Clearnose Skate

Raja eglanteria

RANGE: *Cape Cod to South Florida.*

HABITAT: *Soft bottom near shore.*

DESCRIPTION: Skates are similar in appearance to Stingrays, with the important difference being the absence of the dangerous spike on the tail. Several species are commonly caught—and commonly disliked—by anglers. The Clearnose Skate has transparent "window panes" on either side of its pointed snout. The color is brown or tan, with mottling and a few spots.

SIZE: Average span is about 18 inches; some run to nearly 3 feet.

FOOD VALUE: Good; same as Stingrays.

GAME QUALITIES: Poor.

TACKLE AND BAITS: Any sort of bottom tackle, with dead shrimp or cutbait.

FISHING METHODS: Still Fishing.

Barndoor Skate

Raja laevis

DESCRIPTION: The snout is sharply pointed. Color is brown or rusty with darker blotches and numerous small spots.

SIZE: A large Skate, it averages about 3 feet in span and sometimes exceeds 5 feet.

FOOD VALUE: Very good and sometimes sold commercially.

GAME QUALITIES: Typical of its family, it is not much of a gamester, although it can be tough to raise, especially if hooked in deep water.

TACKLE AND BAITS: All sorts of bottom baits, fished on all sorts of tackle, will take Skates—usually by accident, not plan.

FISHING SYSTEMS: Still Fishing.

OTHER NAMES:

Sharpnose Skate

RANGE: *Newfoundland to Cape Hatteras.*

HABITAT: *Roams from brackish water out to the deep banks, at least 100 feet.*

Winter Skate

Raja ocellata

OTHER NAMES:

Big Skate
Eyed Skate
Spotted Skate

RANGE: *Newfoundland to Cape Hatteras.*

HABITAT: *In northern part of its range it is common inshore during winter, even in near-freezing water. Farther south, its comfort zone is found only in offshore water to 300 feet or more.*

DESCRIPTION: Head and wings are rounded. Color is light or medium brown with many small spots plus one or more ocelli on each wing and on each pectoral fin. (Ocelli are eye-like spots with a circle surrounding a darker center). Translucent areas on each side of the snout are not so large or transparent as in the Clearnose Skate.

SIZE: Averages a couple of feet; reaches at least 3 feet.

GAME QUALITIES: Typical of its family, it is not much of a gamester, although it can be tough to raise.

TACKLE AND BAITS: All sorts of bottom baits, fished on all sorts of tackle, will take Skates.

FISHING SYSTEMS: Still Fishing.

Largetooth Sawfish

Pristis pristis

RANGE: *The Smalltooth extends from Florida to Cape Hatteras and is also found in Bermuda. The Largetooth is found only in Florida.*

HABITAT: *Likes mud or sand bottom along the coast, and will wander far up freshwater streams.*

DESCRIPTION: Sawfish can be described as elongated Rays whose snouts form a "saw" with sharp teeth on both sides. The pictured Largetooth Sawfish and the **Smalltooth Sawfish**, *Pristis pectinata* are now uncommon.

SIZE: Anglers are more apt to encounter small specimens, but world record is 890 pounds, 8 ounces.

FOOD VALUE: None. Protected species.

GAME QUALITIES: Poor, unless very large.

TACKLE AND BAITS: Seldom caught. Occasionally bites dead baits fished for Sharks.

FISHING METHODS: Still Fishing.

Atlantic Torpedo

Torpedo nobiliana

DESCRIPTION: The Torpedo is related to the Rays and Skates but belongs to a different group. Somewhat Skate-like in appearance, its body is round and it has a large lobe on the caudal fin. Color is brown or purplish.

SIZE: Potentially to more than 100 pounds. World record 35 pounds, 4 ounces.

FOOD VALUE: None.

GAME QUALITIES: Nothing you'd like to test.

TACKLE AND BAITS: Feeds on a variety of small fish and shellfish and occasionally takes bottom baits fished for Cod and other groundfish.

FISHING SYSTEMS: Still Fishing.

OTHER NAMES:

Electric Ray

RANGE: *Nova Scotia to South Florida.*

HABITAT: *Fortunately, not very common anywhere. Like all its kin it is a bottom hugger. It frequently comes into shallow water in the North, but nearly always stays very deep in the south.*

Atlantic Guitarfish

Rhinobatos lentiginosus

DESCRIPTION: In addition to being compared to a string instrument, the Guitarfish has been described as half Skate and half Dogfish — the front half being the Skate and the rear half being the Dogfish, or small Shark. Usual color is light brown with small white spots.

SIZE: Seldom exceeds 2 feet in length.

FOOD VALUE: Poor.

GAME QUALITIES: Poor.

TACKLE AND BAITS: Only an oddity, they are occasionally caught by an angler bottom-fishing with small baits.

FISHING SYSTEMS: Still Fishing.

RANGE: *South Florida to North Carolina; straggles a bit farther north.*

HABITAT: *Soft bottom of surf, bays, estuaries and coastal streams.*

Mullets and Mojarras belong to different families, but both inhabit coastal waters and often run into fresh water as well. Only a couple of the larger types in each group are of much interest as hook-and-line targets — and then mostly to shorebound fishermen who patiently set out to capture supper. Far exceeding their rather small role as hook-and-line targets themselves, Mullet are among the chief allies of coastal sport fishermen, thanks to their annual runs, which serve as a moveable feast that concentrates major gamefish of many types — from Striped Bass and Bluefish along northern shores, to Snook and Tarpon off the southern beaches. And all that, of course, is in addition to their value as both fresh and processed bait.

Mullets and Mojarras

Striped Mullet

White Mullet

Liza

Mountain Mullet

Irish Pompano

Yellowfin Mojarra

Striped Mullet

Mugil cephalus

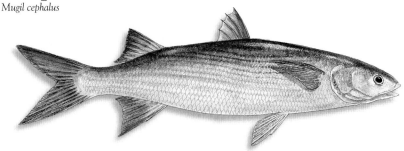

OTHER NAMES:

Black Mullet
Jumping Mullet

RANGE: *Florida to Nova Scotia; most abundant south of Cape Hatteras.*

HABITAT: *Shallow coastal waters and bays; ventures far into fresh water.*

DESCRIPTION: Back and upper sides are dark gray, Lower sides and belly are silvery. Several longitudinal stripes generally apparent. Tail is deeply forked and solid in color.

SIZE: Most run from 1-3 pounds, but 5-pounders are often seen and the maximum is probably 10 pounds. World record 6 pounds, 15 ounces.

FOOD VALUE: Excellent, but depends on personal taste. Flesh is oily and distinctively flavored.

GAME QUALITIES: A wild, surface-cutting fighter.

TACKLE AND BAITS: A cast net is by far the best bet for catching Black Mullet, since all Mullet primarily feed on algae and do not bite in the usual sense. They will, however, take a small bait into their mouth briefly as they forage, and many are caught by patient cane-pole fishermen in coastal streams or canals. Baits are many and include bits of white plastic worm, real earthworms, corn kernels, dabs of bacon and some other odds and ends. It's possible to catch Mullet by fly casting in situations where the fish can be seen as they mouth floating vegetable matter or grasses on bottom. A small fly cast to their vicinity is often picked up, but the angler must be alert and ready to set the hook instantly, before the fly is expelled.

FISHING SYSTEMS: Still Fishing.

White Mullet

Mugil curema

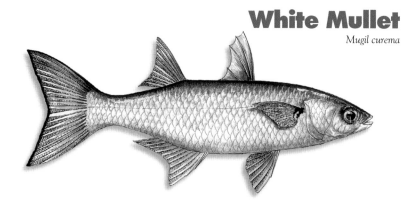

DESCRIPTION: Silver Mullet are generally smaller than Blacks and lighter in color. The stripes are also less noticeable, or absent. The tail is not so deeply forked, but the most obvious distinguishing feature is that the rear edges of the tail are edged in black.

SIZE: Averages a pound or less but can exceed 3 pounds. World record 1 pound, 2 ounces.

FOOD VALUE: Equal to the Black Mullet, though not often eaten.

GAME QUALITIES: A good fighter for its size.

TACKLE AND BAITS: Silver Mullet are never fished for selectively, but can be caught on the same baits recommended for Black Mullet. The smaller Silvers are used primarily for bait—live or cut—and most are caught by cast netting or (where legal) by gill netting and seining.

FISHING SYSTEMS: Still Fishing.

OTHER NAMES:

Silver Mullet
Lisa Blanca
Liseta

RANGE: *Florida to New England. It is also the common Mullet of Bermuda.*

HABITAT: *Shallow coastal waters. Roams into fresh water. One of the two major species of Mullet, along with the Striped variety, involved in annual "Mullet runs."*

Liza

Mugil liza

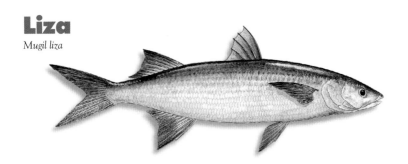

OTHER NAMES:

Caribbean Mullet

RANGE: *Bermuda and South Florida.*

HABITAT: *Shallow shorelines of coast and bays; some in fresh water.*

DESCRIPTION: Very difficult to distinguish from the Black Mullet by visual inspection, the main difference being a narrower and more pointed head.

SIZE: Common at 6-12 inches and grows to about 2 feet. World record 3 pounds, 3 ounces.

FOOD VALUE: Same as other Mullet.

GAME QUALITIES: Again, cannot be fished for selectively, but they are very much the same as Black Mullet in size and habit, though far less common in Florida.

TACKLE AND BAITS: Nets.

FISHING SYSTEMS: Cast netting.

Mountain Mullet

Agonostomus monticola

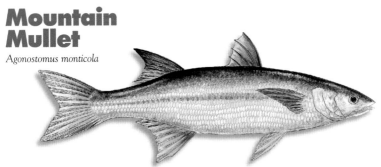

RANGE: *Florida to North Carolina, but not common.*

HABITAT: *Mostly in rivers, but also coastal. The "Mountain" name originated in Jamaica, where there is a fishery for them in mountain streams.*

DESCRIPTION: A yellow tail and more yellow on the dorsal and anal fins distinguish this Mullet. The head is also sharply pointed, and there usually is a dark stripe.

SIZE: Around 12 inches; seldom larger.

FOOD VALUE: Very good.

GAME QUALITIES: Fast and spirited fighter.

TACKLE AND BAITS: Although they are seldom caught in this country, ultralight spinning and light fly outfits, with tiny spinners or various wet flies, work.

FISHING SYSTEMS: Casting; Still Fishing.

Irish Pompano
Diapterus auratus

DESCRIPTION: The deep body is greenish or grayish above, white or silvery on sides and belly. The second spines of both the dorsal and anal fins are very long and rigid. The lips are telescopic and can be extended outward and downward.

SIZE: Up to 1 foot in length.

FOOD VALUE: A good panfish.

GAME QUALITIES: Fun on light line.

TACKLE AND BAITS: Seldom fished for except by youngsters, who catch them from bayside docks and along shorelines on poles or light spinning tackle.

FISHING SYSTEMS: Still Fishing.

OTHER NAMES:

Mojarra
Shad
Punchmouth

RANGE: *South Florida.*

HABITAT: *Shallow, protected waters with mud or sand bottom. Travels far up freshwater rivers.*

Yellowfin Mojarra
Gerres cinereus

DESCRIPTION: Body shape is quite similar to that of the Irish Pompano, but it is usually darker and more vividly marked. Color is brownish or olive on the back and silvery on the sides. Dark bars are apparent on the sides. The pelvic fins are yellow.

SIZE: Larger than the Irish Pompano. Often exceeds a pound in weight. World record 1 pound, 3 ounces.

FOOD VALUE: A good panfish.

GAME QUALITIES: Pretty tough for its size.

TACKLE AND BAITS: Poles or ultralight and light spinning outfits. Takes many kinds of cutbaits.

FISHING SYSTEMS: Still Fishing.

OTHER NAMES:

Shad
Punchmouth

RANGE: *Florida and Bermuda.*

HABITAT: *Prefers clear water of protected beaches, shorelines, shallow reefs and grassflats.*

Fish that school heavily are key links in the oceanic food chain — and they are important to sport fishermen in more ways than that. The Shads are eagerly chased by sportsmen from Canada to Florida, besides which they join their close relatives, the Atlantic and Blueback Herrings, in being famous as table fare. As for the rest of the species in this chapter, many are certainly edible and commercially important, but it's of more interest to sport fishermen that, collectively, they comprise one of the primary sources of live bait, frozen bait and chum for anglers all along the Atlantic coast. Most "baitfishes" are in the Herring family, but here several other popular bait species are lumped with them.

Chapter

22

Herrings
and
Baitfishes

American Shad

Hickory Shad

Gizzard Shad

Alewife

Atlantic Herring

Blueback Herring

Atlantic Menhaden

Scaled Sardine

Atlantic Thread Herring

Spanish Sardine

Atlantic Smelt

Butterfish

American Sand Lance

Atlantic Silverside

Mummichog

Bay Anchovy

Ballyhoo

Bigeye Scad

Round Scad

Redtail Scad

American Shad

Alosa sapidissima

OTHER NAMES:

Common Shad

RANGE: *Nova Scotia to Florida's St. Johns River.*

HABITAT: *Many large rivers on the Atlantic Coast enjoy runs of Shad, which live at sea but return to spawn in spring.*

DESCRIPTION: A dark spot just aft of the gill cover near the back is followed by a series of smaller black dots. Color is green above with silvery sides and a sharp ridge on the belly. The fins are soft.

SIZE: Most run 1-4 pounds. World record 11 pounds.

FOOD VALUE: Shad fillets are very good, but bony.

GAME QUALITIES: Nicknamed "freshwater Tarpon," Shad are terrific battlers and very acrobatic.

TACKLE AND BAITS: Most Shad are taken with spinning or light baitcasting tackle, but they have a devoted legion of fly fishermen as well.

FISHING SYSTEMS: Trolling; Casting.

Hickory Shad

Alosa mediocris

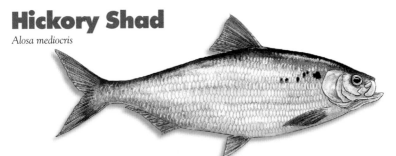

OTHER NAMES:

Fall Herring

RANGE: *Nova Scotia to North Florida.*

HABITAT: *This Shad is also a sea dweller that spawns in the rivers. It prefers small tributaries, but a few do mix with American Shad in the main rivers.*

DESCRIPTION: Although it looks very much like the American Shad, it does not attain large size and can be distinguished by the lower jaw, longer than the upper.

SIZE: Averages around 1 pound; some hit 3 pounds.

FOOD VALUE: Good but bony.

GAME QUALITIES: Outstanding for its size.

TACKLE AND BAITS: Although seldom targeted, the Hickory Shad can be taken on the same small lures and flies used for their larger relatives. Often caught incidentally while fishing for Perch, Crappie or Bass.

FISHING SYSTEMS: Trolling; Casting; Drifting.

Gizzard Shad

Dorosoma cepedianum

DESCRIPTION: Smaller and rounder than the preceding Shads. Color is similar but a thread-like final ray of the dorsal fin is the giveaway. Also, there are spots inside and outside the mouth.

SIZE: Average length is 2-6 inches; a few top 10 inches. World record 4 pounds, 6 ounces.

FOOD VALUE: None. Only value is as bait.

GAME QUALITIES: None.

TACKLE AND BAITS: Not caught on sporting tackle.

FISHING SYSTEMS: Cast netting.

RANGE: *Estuaries and rivers of the entire Atlantic Coast, in both brackish and fresh water.*

HABITAT: *Prefers open water over mud bottom, but roams widely.*

Alewife

Alosa pseudoharengus

DESCRIPTION: Again, typical Herring coloration—blue or green above; silvery on sides. A spot usually is located just behind the gill cover on line with the eye. Lower jaw does not extend beyond upper jaw when mouth is closed.

SIZE: 10-12 inches on average; reaches 16 inches or so.

FOOD VALUE: Very good. Sold fresh, smoked and canned. Rivals the Common Herring.

GAME QUALITIES: None.

TACKLE AND BAITS: Occasionally caught by accident on tiny baits.

FISHING SYSTEMS: Netting.

OTHER NAMES:

Freshwater Herring

RANGE: *Labrador to Cape Hatteras; straggles to North Florida.*

HABITAT: *Nearshore waters, invading rivers to spawn in quiet tributaries or lakes. Landlocked in Great Lakes and some other large northern lakes.*

Atlantic Herring

Clupea harengus

OTHER NAMES:

Common Herring
Sardine

RANGE: *Labrador to New York; sometimes to Cape Hatteras.*

HABITAT: *Open water from near the coast to offshore.*

DESCRIPTION: The body is elongated. Color is green to blue on the back with silvery sides and thin abdomen. That coloration is generally the same for most Herrings, but this one wears its dorsal fin amidships, which is farther back than the others.

SIZE: Around 12 inches; maximum about 18 inches.

FOOD VALUE: One of the best commercially. Sold fresh, pickled, smoked and canned (small ones are the fish most often sold as "Sardines").

GAME QUALITIES: Not important, but scrappy.

TACKLE AND BAITS: Seldom fished for with line.

FISHING SYSTEMS: Netting; Still Fishing.

Blueback Herring

Alosa aestivalis

OTHER NAMES:

Summer Herring
Blue Herring

RANGE: *Gulf of St. Lawrence to North Florida.*

HABITAT: *Open sea, entering estuaries and river mouths in spawning season.*

DESCRIPTION: Blue back and silvery sides. Faint stripes are really raised scales. Small spot behind gill cover.

SIZE: Less than a foot on average; reaches about 14 inches.

FOOD VALUE: Good, but not nearly as prominent a food fish as the Common Herring.

GAME QUALITIES: Fun on lightest tackle.

TACKLE AND BAITS: Not a sport fish but can occasionally be caught by adults for bait, or by youngsters for fun, on tiny hooks baited with pieces of squid, shrimp or fish.

FISHING SYSTEMS: Still Fishing.

Atlantic Menhaden

Brevoortia tyrannus

DESCRIPTION: Two or three species of Menhaden are similar in size and appearance, and interchangeable in their bait appeal. The Atlantic Menhaden is slightly larger than the others and more widely distributed.

SIZE: To about 12 inches. Average is around 8.

FOOD VALUE: Very oily. Best used for bait.

GAME QUALITIES: The Menhadens are strong for their size, which makes them ideal for bait.

TACKLE AND BAITS: Most are cast netted.

FISHING SYSTEMS: Still Fishing; Drift Fishing.

OTHER NAMES:

Mossbunker
Bunker
Pogy
Fatback

RANGE: *Nova Scotia to Florida.*

HABITAT: *Ranges widely in open water, but is most often sought by anglers fairly close to the beaches, or around shoals and wrecks.*

Scaled Sardine

Harengula jaguana

DESCRIPTION: The Scaled Sardine is the most common of several species that Florida anglers lump together under the names "Pilchard" or "Whitebait." The similar **Redear Sardine**, *Harengula humeralis* and **False Pilchard**, *Harengula clupeola* also occur in South Florida but are less common. Both have an orange spot on the gill cover.

SIZE: Averages 3-6 inches.

FOOD VALUE: Insignificant.

GAME QUALITIES: None.

TACKLE AND BAITS: Most are cast netted, but they can also be caught with multi-hook bait rigs.

FISHING SYSTEMS: Still Fishing.

OTHER NAMES:

Pilchard
Whitebait

RANGE: *Florida.*

HABITAT: *Roams widely in both shallow and deep water. Bait-seekers look for them inshore on grassy flats or around bridge or pier pilings and navigation aids. Offshore, they frequently congregate near structure.*

Atlantic Thread Herring

Opisthonema oglinum

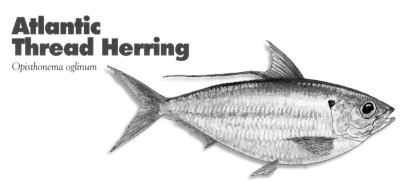

OTHER NAMES:

Greenie
Shiner
Thread
Machuelo

RANGE: *New England to Florida; also Bermuda.*

HABITAT: *Both inshore and off-shore waters.*

DESCRIPTION: Body is deeper than that of Sardines or "Pilchards," but the most distinguishing feature is the elongated, threadlike posterior ray of the dorsal fin. It also is more widely distributed along the coast. The back is green and the sides silvery with several dark, lengthwise streaks. Dark spot behind gill cover.

SIZE: Averages 4-6 inches; maximum about 12 inches.

FOOD VALUE: Seldom eaten.

GAME QUALITIES: None.

TACKLE AND BAITS: Usually caught in cast nets, but also on multi-hooked bait rigs.

FISHING SYSTEMS: Still Fishing.

Spanish Sardine

Sardinella aurita

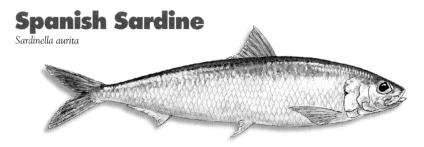

OTHER NAMES:

Sardine
Shiner

RANGE: *New England to Florida.*

HABITAT: *Common on inshore flats, but occurs in deep water too.*

DESCRIPTION: Body is more elongated and more rounded than in other Herrings. Silver sides and green back with no markings. A similar species, the **Orange-spot Sardine, *Sardinella brasiliensis*,** has a gold streak on the side.

SIZE: Averages 2-4 inches; reaches 10.

FOOD VALUE: Good, but seldom eaten.

GAME QUALITIES: None.

TACKLE AND BAITS: Will respond to chum and can then be cast netted or taken on tiny hooks.

FISHING SYSTEMS: Still Fishing.

Atlantic Smelt

Osmerus mordax

DESCRIPTION: Green or brown above, silvery below, often with a streak of darker silver down the side from gill to tail.

SIZE: Averages 8-12 inches; sometimes slightly larger.

FOOD VALUE: Excellent fresh, if kept well iced. Also good when pickled or smoked.

GAME QUALITIES: Too small to be a challenge, but cooperative and fun.

TACKLE AND BAITS: The lightest rods and lines, with tiny hooks and bits of shrimp or marine worms for bait.

FISHING SYSTEMS: Still Fishing.

OTHER NAMES:

Rainbow Smelt
Arctic Smelt

RANGE: *Labrador to New York; straggles to Maryland.*

HABITAT: *Stays close to shore and enters rivers to spawn. Most recreational catches are made in bays and river mouths.*

Butterfish

Peprilus triacanthus

DESCRIPTION: Rounded shape with deeply forked tail. Back is greenish; sides silver with many small spots.

SIZE: Average is 4-6 inches; may reach 12 inches.

FOOD VALUE: Very good but oily. Anglers use them mostly for bait, and also for chum, either ground or in chunks for Tuna fishing.

GAME QUALITIES: Poor.

TACKLE AND BAITS: Most are netted, but they can be caught on small hooks with a variety of cutbaits.

FISHING SYSTEMS: Netting; Still Fishing.

RANGE: *Newfoundland to Florida; more plentiful in northern areas.*

HABITAT: *From near shore to the open sea.*

American Sand Lance

Ammodytes americanus

OTHER NAMES:

Sand Eel
Lancefish

RANGE: *Labrador to Cape Hatteras.*

HABITAT: *Sandy beaches and shorelines. It hides by burrowing several inches deep in soft sand.*

DESCRIPTION: Slender and round-bodied, the Sand Lance resembles a small Eel, but an obvious point of distinction is the forked tail, which is separate from the dorsal and anal fins. Color is brownish above, silvery below, often with a blue stripe on the side.

SIZE: Up to about 6 inches.

FOOD VALUE: Good but seldom eaten. Used mostly as bait.

GAME QUALITIES: Nil.

TACKLE AND BAITS: Not sought with hook and line.

FISHING SYSTEMS: Can be dug from the sand at water's edge along many shorelines.

Atlantic Silverside

Menidia menidia

OTHER NAMES:

Spearing
Sand Smelt
Shiner
Rainfish
Glass Minnow

RANGE: *Gulf of St. Lawrence to Florida; also Bermuda.*

HABITAT: *Atlantic Silversides along shores and river mouths; others offshore and over reefs.*

DESCRIPTION: Superficially similar to other schooling baitfishes such as the Anchovies and Smelt, Silversides can be distinguished from either by the much smaller mouth. Several closely similar species are, again, all the same to most anglers. Color is generally olive above, white below, with a silver streak from gill to tail. The Atlantic Silverside also has numerous small dots.

SIZE: Averages 2-4 inches; may reach 6 inches.

FOOD VALUE: Good, but the major use is for chum.

GAME QUALITIES: Nil.

TACKLE AND BAITS: Not taken on hook and line.

FISHING SYSTEMS: Netting.

Mummichog
Fundulus heteroclitus

DESCRIPTION: The blunt-headed Mummichog is probably the most familiar of many types of Killifishes, frequently used as bait for everything from Flounder to Weakfish and Red Drum. All have square or fanlike tails and some have fanlike dorsal fins as well. Color is usually mottled brown, often with stripes.

SIZE: Most run 2-4 inches. Maximum is about 6 inches.

FOOD VALUE: Good but seldom eaten.

GAME QUALITIES: Poor.

TACKLE AND BAITS: Can be caught with tiny hooks and bits of cut bait.

FISHING SYSTEMS: Still Fishing; Netting; Trapping.

OTHER NAMES:

Killifish
Mud Minnow
Marsh Minnow
Chub

RANGE: Entire Atlantic Coast from Labrador to Florida.

HABITAT: Always found in calm and protected waters — bays, estuaries, coastal creeks and into fresh water.

Bay Anchovy
Anchoa mitchilli

DESCRIPTION: Several species of Anchovies are viewed as one by anglers along the Atlantic Coast. This is the most common. The Anchovies are characterized by a proportionately wide and underslung mouth. Most of them, especially the smaller specimens, are translucent, hence the name "Glass Minnow."

SIZE: Average is 1-4 inches.

FOOD VALUE: As with canned Anchovies, edible but debatable. Anglers use them mostly for chum.

GAME QUALITIES: None.

TACKLE AND BAITS: Beach seines; dipnets; cast nets.

FISHING SYSTEMS: Netting.

OTHER NAMES:

Glass Minnow
Fry
Bigmouth Fry

RANGE: Maine to Florida; also Bermuda.

HABITAT: Most are found in shallow water and along shorelines, but some occur far offshore.

Ballyhoo

Hemiramphus brasiliensis

OTHER NAMES:

Balao

Halfbeak

RANGE: *Maine to Florida; also Bermuda.*

HABITAT: *Most common around reefs and shoals, but widespread from deep water to larger bays.*

DESCRIPTION: Differs from Needlefish in that only the lower jaw is elongated into a "bill." Several species occur but two are prominent. Their ranges overlap. Ballyhoo, shown here, has a short pectoral fin. The **Balao,** *Hemiramphus balao* has a long pectoral fin.

SIZE: Both species average 10 inches, but reach 15.

FOOD VALUE: Not bad, but seldom eaten.

GAME QUALITIES: Cagey biters and zippy little fighters, but too small except as bait.

TACKLE AND BAITS: Ballyhoo respond readily to ground chum.

FISHING SYSTEMS: Still Fishing.

Bigeye Scad

Selar crumenophthalmus

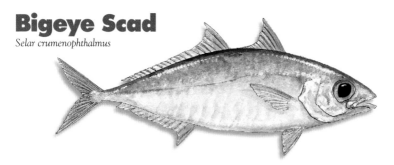

OTHER NAMES:

Goggle-eye

RANGE: *Nova Scotia to Florida; also Bermuda.*

HABITAT: *Reefs and other outside waters; also in and near inlets. Also enters river mouths and bays.*

DESCRIPTION: The body is cylindrical and tail forked. Color is steel blue. Very large eye.

SIZE: Less than one foot.

FOOD VALUE: Good, but usually used for bait.

GAME QUALITIES: Good fighter for its size.

TACKLE AND BAITS: Most Goggle-eyes are caught at night, either deliberately as potential bait, or accidentally while chumming and bottom fishing. Bait fishermen tempt their Goggle-eyes with small jigs.

FISHING SYSTEMS: Still Fishing; Casting.

Round Scad

Decapterus punctatus

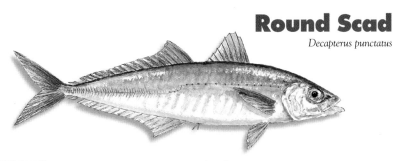

DESCRIPTION: Color is dull gray or tan with white underparts and small black spots along the lateral line. The body is cigar-shaped. The tail is forked and scutes are present.

SIZE: Averages 6-8 inches.

FOOD VALUE: Used as bait, not food.

GAME QUALITIES: None.

TACKLE AND BAITS: Although anglers purchase most of their Cigar Minnows in fresh or frozen state, they can be caught on bait rigs — a series of tiny hooks that are sometimes dressed with nylon filaments.

FISHING SYSTEMS: Drifting; Still Fishing.

OTHER NAMES:

Cigar Minnow

RANGE: *Nova Scotia to Florida; also Bermuda.*

HABITAT: *Large schools are widespread, from near the beaches to well offshore.*

Redtail Scad

Decapterus tabl

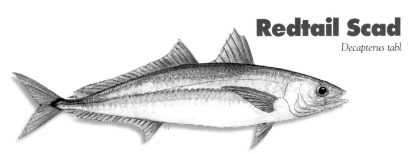

DESCRIPTION: Tail is bright red and very noticeable in the water. Similar in shape to the Cigar Minnow.

SIZE: Averages 12-14 inches.

FOOD VALUE: Edible but seldom put on the table.

GAME QUALITIES: Often a challenge to hook, but no great shakes as a fighter because of small size.

TACKLE AND BAITS: To catch Speedos as bait for King Mackerel and other gamefish, try your lightest spinning outfit with a hair hook and bits of ground chum as bait.

FISHING SYSTEMS: Still Fishing.

OTHER NAMES:

Speedo

RANGE: *Cape Hatteras to Florida; also Bermuda.*

HABITAT: *Widespread in open offshore waters.*

Index

Don't Miss These Books

Baits, Rigs & Tackle

The number-one selling fishing how-to book of all time with over 300,000 in print, recently updated. Fishing legend and Florida Sportsman Senior Editor Vic Dunaway tells exactly what is needed to get rigged and ready to catch fish. ISBN # 0-936240-14-8.
$11.95

From Hook to Table

More vintage Vic Dunaway, informing readers of all aspects involved in preparing and cooking seafood. The book, with a newly designed cover is full of how-to illustrations and over 100 mouthwatering recipes. ISBN # 0-936240-15-6.
$9.95

Consider the Source

The important thing about any fish story is to think about who's telling it.

When that source is Vic Dunaway, all veteran anglers' ears perk up.

Vic is trusted, for good reason. He's done his homework, he's been there, for more years than most of us have existed.

That's why Vic is the ideal author to handle this long-awaited Sport Fish of the Atlantic.

From his many network TV appearances and best-selling books to his years of editing Florida Sportsman Magazine, the name Vic Dunaway amounts to a seal of authenticity. You know you're getting the straight scoop from someone who's studied fish in research channels and, importantly, in that big wet lab where fast currents flow.

Vic lives in Florida, but like the fish he loves to catch, he's always ready to travel to the next hotspot a thousand miles up the stream.

As a perfect complement to Vic's text, the original illustrations of Kevin R. Brant, many of which have appeared in companion books to this one, accompany information about each species.

Editor Eric Wickstrom and Artist Karen Miller round out the foursome putting together this volume that we trust you will have ready the next time your reel sizzles with action.